Table of Contents

I0393857

Table of Contents (Continued)

2012 WORKPLACE AND GENDER RELATIONS SURVEY OF ACTIVE DUTY MEMBERS: NONRESPONSE BIAS ANALYSIS REPORT

Introduction and Outline

The Defense Manpower Data Center (DMDC) conducted several studies to assess the presence of nonresponse bias in estimates from the *2012 Workplace and Gender Relations Survey of Active Duty Members (2012 WGRA)*.

The objective of this research was to assess the extent of nonresponse bias for the estimated rate of unwanted sexual contact (USC rate)[1] in the active duty military. The level of nonresponse bias (NRB) can vary for every question on the survey, but DMDC focused on the USC rate because this is the central question on the survey. Nonresponse bias occurs when survey respondents are systematically different from the nonrespondents. Nonresponse bias can occur with high or low survey response rates, but the decrease in survey response rates in the past decade has resulted in a greater focus on potential NRB. DMDC investigated the presence of nonresponse bias using many different methods, and this paper summarizes the following methods and results:

1. Analyze response rates from *2012 WGRA* and other DMDC surveys,

2. Evaluate composition of sample compared with survey respondents,

3. Assess how effectively DMDC weighting reduces nonresponse bias,

4. Use late respondents as a proxy for nonrespondents,

5. Use hard-to-reach (HTR) respondents as a proxy for nonrespondents,

6. Analyze item missing data for USC question,

7. Analyze whether past USC victims' respond to later WGRA surveys at different rates.

The first section of this paper is a summary of DMDCs nonresponse bias results. The second section describes the *2012 WGRA* survey. The third section consists of the individual

---

[1] In the past 12 months, have you experienced any of the following intentional sexual contacts that were against your will or occurred when you did not or could not consent where someone...
  - Sexually touched you (e.g., intentional touching of genitalia, breasts, or buttocks) or made you sexually touch them?
  - Attempted to make you have sexual intercourse, but was not successful?
  - Made you have sexual intercourse?
  - Attempted to make you perform or receive oral sex, anal sex, or penetration by a finger or object, but was not successful?
  - Made you perform or receive oral sex, anal sex, or penetration by a finger or object?

nonresponse bias studies. The fourth section consists of recommendations for further model-based research. The final section contains additional appendix tables.

Summary of Findings

Nonresponse bias (NRB) is difficult to assess. Most authors recommend averaging across several different studies to measure NRB. We have taken that approach here and conducted seven studies to assess NRB in USC estimates. **Our analyses indicate that it is unlikely that the *2012 WGRA* overestimates the USC rate, and there is some evidence that the survey underestimates the USC rate, although the level of nonresponse bias appears to be modest**.

We summarize the results from each study below:

1. **Analyze response rates from *2012 WGRA* and other DMDC surveys**—Analysis of response rates show that comparisons of WGRA and the *Status of Forces Survey of Active Duty Members* (SOFS-A) provide evidence that topic saliency does not substantially alter response rates to the WGRA survey, and therefore any increase in NRB over the SOFS-A is likely to be small to modest.

2. **Evaluate composition of sample compared with survey respondents**—The WGRA sample composition demographically differs from the active duty population distribution due to intentional sampling strategies that allow DMDC to make precise estimates for small subgroups. The respondent composition differs from the sample distribution in predictable ways due to subgroups (e.g., junior enlisted) responding at different rates. Analyses show that the survey weights effectively eliminate these differences and the distribution of weighted survey respondents closely matches the active duty population.

3. **Assess how effectively DMDC weighting reduces nonresponse bias**—Analysis of DMDC's weighting methods shows that the variables used during weighting effectively reduce nonresponse bias in the USC estimates. Active duty members have different response propensities and different USC rates for response categories of the weighting variables, and therefore weighting that aligns respondents with known active duty distributions reduces nonresponse bias.

4. **Use late respondents as a proxy for nonrespondents**—The analysis of late respondents provides no systematic evidence of nonresponse bias in the estimates of the USC rate. Late respondents are disproportionately from low response rate groups and groups that have higher USC rates, and therefore we would expect unweighted USC rates to be higher for late respondents. After separately reweighting early and late respondents, the late respondents have slightly lower USC rates, although the difference is very small. We recommend cautious interpretation of these results because of the unexpected difference by gender (late females reported higher USC while late males reported lower USC).

5. **Use hard-to-reach (HTR) respondents as a proxy for nonrespondents**—HTR respondents are disproportionately E1-E4, Marine Corps, and males; E1-E4 and Marine Corps are groups that have higher USC rates, and therefore we would expected unweighted USC rates to be higher for HTR respondents. After separately reweighting HTR and regular respondents, HTR and regular respondents have very similar overall USC rates.

6. **Analyze item missing data for USC question**—The small level of item missing data on the USC question and insignificant number of drop-offs at the USC question provide evidence that the sensitive nature of the USC question did not deter members from providing answers. Our analysis of missing data provides no evidence of nonresponse bias.

7. **Analyze whether past USC victims' respond to later WGRA surveys at different rates**—Members who reported experiencing USC in an earlier survey appear less likely to respond to later WGRA surveys. This provides limited evidence that USC victims may be less likely to participate in WGRA surveys and suggests the WGRA may underestimate USC rates. Based on our analysis, we anticipate this impact to be minimal.

2012 WGRA Production Survey

The *2012 WGRA* survey sample size was 108,478 active duty members selected from the 1,372,971 active members on the *April 2012 Active Duty Master File (ADMF)*. The frame included Army, Navy, Marine Corps, and Air Force active duty members who were ranked E1-O6 in April and were at least 18 years old on August 1, 2012 when the survey fielded. DMDC selected a stratified random sample using the following five characteristics to define the stratification dimensions: Service, gender, paygrade,[2] race/ethnicity[3] and deployment status.[4] There were 22,792 eligible sampled members that returned completed surveys resulting in a 24.1% weighted response rate. We weighted these respondents to the full active population using standard, weighting methods. The four-step weighting process included:

1. Assigning a base weight based on the inverse of the probability of selection,

2. Adjusting the current weight by eligibility,

3. Adjusting the current weight by completion,

4. Post-stratifying the current weight to known population totals for Service, gender, paygrade, and race.

---

[2] Paygrade was stratified as a seven level variable: E1-E3, E4, E5-E6, E7-E9, W1-W5, O1-O3, O4-O6
[3] Race/ethnicity was stratified as a two level variable: Minority/Non-Minority
[4] Deployment was stratified as a three level variable: Never Deployed, Deployed but not in past 12 months, Deployed in past 12 months

Based on this statistical process DMDC estimated that overall 1.9% (±0.4[5]) of active duty military members had experienced unwanted sexual contact (USC) in the last 12 months. DMDC further estimated that 6.1% of females (±0.6) and 1.2% of males (±0.4) in the active duty military had experienced USC in the last 12 months. The statistical methodology report (DMDC, 2012b) provides more details regarding the sampling, weighting, and variance estimation and the tabulation volume (DMDC, 2012c) provides details for the estimates of USC rates by additional demographic groups.

---

[5] The margin of error of this estimate is based on a 95 percent confidence interval

Section I:
Analyze Response Rates From 2012 WGRA and Other DMDC Surveys

DMDC always computes response rates by many known geographic and demographic variables (e.g., Service and paygrade). Differential response rates can be evidence of potential NRB unless these variables are controlled for during survey weighting. Table 1 shows that response rates to the WGRA vary greatly by subgroup; for example, O4-O6's consistently respond at a much higher rate than E1-E4's. Because O4-O6's also report very different USC rates than E1-E4's, NRB levels would be high if DMDC used unweighted estimates. However, DMDC controls for Service, paygrade, gender, race, deployment, family status, combat status, and other characteristics that are correlated with response propensity as well as actual survey responses (e.g., USC), when constructing survey weights. Therefore, analysis of response rates alone does not provide evidence of NRB in weighted WGRA estimates. Instead, the focus of this response rate analysis is to assess a different hypothesis. Some critics have hypothesized that women, or potentially USC victims, would be more likely to respond to the WGRA because of the subject matter, a hypothesis Groves (2000) refers to as topic saliency. If this were true, women should respond at different rates to the WGRA than they do to other active duty surveys that do not focus on gender issues.

To assess this hypothesis, DMDC compared the *2012 WGRA* response rates to previously fielded WGRA surveys and recent SOFS-A. The SOFS-A is DMDC's main recurring general topic survey that covers the same active duty population as WGRA. DMDC used the two prior WGRA surveys (*2010 WGRA* and *2006 WGRA*) and the SOFS-A surveys that fielded the closest to the WGRA surveys. Two SOFS-A were conducted in 2012 and one SOFS-A was done in 2010 and 2011.[6] The 2006 SOFS-A (*August 2006 SOFS-A*) was closest in fielding to the *2006 WGRA*. Table 1 shows overall response rates (labeled "Total") and response rates for key demographic subgroups.

Table 1 shows that response rates to the WGRA follow patterns consistent with known trends in the SOFS-A. Over time, across all military surveys, active duty response rates have steadily declined. The WGRA shows a more severe decline than the SOFS-A; however, this can be attributed to budget pressures that forced the removal of the WGRA paper survey option after the 2010 cycle[7] and the oversurveying of this population on this topic over the last few years.[8]

---

[6] DMDC labels these surveys as *February 2012 SOFS-A, June 2012 SOFS-A, January 2011 SOFS-A,* and *June 2010 SOFS-A*.

[7] The *2006* and *2010 WGRA* surveys had paper and Web response options while the 2012 survey was Web-only. DMDC conducted experiments on the *2010 WGRA* where a random subgroup was Web-only to determine the effects of offering a paper survey. Responses to the survey (e.g., USC) for the paper and Web combination were determined to be sufficiently similar to Web-only to allow removal of the paper survey.

[8] Since 2010, DMDC estimates at least 12 large military surveys (either conducted or scheduled to be conducted) included an assessment of sexual assault of Service members. This does not include civilian surveys of military members (e.g., Centers for Disease Control and Prevention), or command climate surveys (e.g., DEOCS).

Table 1.
Comparison of Trends in WGRA and SOFS-A Response Rates (Shown in Percent)

Key Surveys	WGRA			SOFS-A			
	2012[a]	2010	2006	Jun 2012[b]	Feb 2012[c]	Jun 2010	Aug 2006
Total	24.1	31.8	29.9	26.2	19.9	25.3	28.3
Gender							
Female	28.6	37.4	33.2	28.7	21.4	29.5	27.0
Male	23.3	30.9	29.4	25.7	19.7	24.6	28.6
Service							
Army	17.8	26.1	29.6	19.6	15.6	19.3	30.1
Navy	22.6	32.7	30.4	27.2	19.9	26.3	29.0
Marine Corps	21.1	22.3	17.0	20.5	14.8	18.7	16.5
Air Force	37.7	43.5	35.0	36.9	30.4	38.2	31.3
Paygrade							
E1-E4	12.5	16.9	14.5	13.2	8.8	14.5	13.2
E5-E9	31.0	40.1	38.1	32.7	26.3	30.7	36.3
O1-O3	32.8	44.5	42.5	37.6	27.5	37.0	40.0
O4-O6	45.8	59.7	57.9	54.0	44.4	46.3	56.5

[a]The *2006* and *2010 WGRA* surveys had paper and Web response options while the 2012 survey was Web-only.
[b]DMDC conducted two Status of Forces active duty surveys in 2012.
[c]*February 2012 SOFS-A* (Feb 2012 as shown in the table) had a survey contact experiment where a subset of the sampled members received e-mail only contact and this reduced the overall response rate.

For gender, females consistently respond to active duty surveys at higher rates than males. However, the gender gap is slightly larger for WGRA surveys than for SOFS-A surveys, indicating that the subject matter may influence some females to respond (topic saliency) or may dissuade some males from responding. One hypothesized argument is that males may think "this is a women's survey and does not apply to me." However, these response rates seem to refute that argument because only a very small fraction of male respondents reported a USC (about 1%), but the male response rates still look very similar to SOFS-A surveys. The increase in the gender gap is a consideration but does not necessarily indicate an increase in NRB because gender is a characteristic that is controlled for during survey weighting. Therefore the only way that the larger gender gap could create larger NRB is if the females that were influenced to respond had higher (or lower) USC rates, and that is not testable in these data. However, the presence of this gender gap could lead to slightly increased risk for NRB in WGRA surveys.

For Service, response rate patterns are consistent between the SOFS-A and WGRA surveys across years. Air Force response rates are highest, followed by Navy, and the lowest response rates belong to Army and Marine Corps.[9] The Navy experienced the largest decrease in response rates between the *2010 WGRA* and the *2012 WGRA,* which may be due to separate Navy surveys on gender issues. The response rates by Service provide no evidence of additional NRB in the WGRA survey that does not exist in the SOFS-A.

---

[9] Marine Corps response rates are higher than normal in *2012 WGRA* due to the inclusion of Marines Online as a survey contact method in addition to our standard postal and e-mail contacts.

For paygrade, response rate patterns are consistent across all surveys (see Table 1) where senior officers (O4-O6) respond at the highest rates and response rates decrease as active members become more junior until dropping off rapidly for the junior enlisted (E1-E4). DMDC's weighting methods correct for bias associated with the differential response probabilities for these known characteristics (e.g., Service, paygrade). The response rates by paygrade provide no evidence of additional NRB in the WGRA survey that does not exist in the SOFS-A.

Summary of Response Rates Analysis From 2012 WGRA and Other DMDC Surveys

Comparisons of WGRA and SOFS-A response rates provide evidence that topic saliency does not substantially alter response rates to the WGRA survey, and therefore any increase in NRB, compared to that of a SOFS-A, is likely to be small to modest. However, although WGRA and SOFS-A response rates have similar patterns, the difference between female and male response rates (gender gap) suggests that topic saliency may increase the level of NRB in the WGRA over the SOFS-A, but because the gender gap is only slightly larger for WGRAs, the increase in NRB is likely small.

Section II:
Evaluate Composition of Sample
Compared With Survey Respondents

DMDC next considered whether NRB could occur in a survey that does not have adequate coverage or is not representative of the military population. In this section DMDC evaluates the composition of the *2012 WGRA*, exploring key military demographic breakdowns by survey subgroups (e.g., population total, sample size, respondents, and weighted respondents). DMDC draws optimized samples to reduce survey burden on members as well as produce high levels of precision for important domain estimates by using known information about the military population. It is important to note that DMDC samples are often not proportional to their population. Depending on the specific subgroup, DMDC will over or under sample that group to provide enough responses to make statistically accurate estimates. While the sample and the number of responses might look out of alignment with the population, this is by design. DMDC is able to use its military personnel data to correctly weight the respondents in order to make survey estimates representative of the active duty population. The military demographics considered include: Service, paygrade, gender, and race. Table 2 through Table 5 contains both the frequency and percent for each survey subgroup by demographic category.

Table 2 shows the survey subgroup breakdown by Service. At the request of the Marine Corps, DMDC sampled more Marine Corps members for the *2012 WGRA* (24% of the population versus 49% of the sample). Based on historically higher response rates, DMDC under sampled the Air Force (11% of the sample versus 14% of the population) and Navy (17% of the sample versus 23% of the population). Due to the large size of the Army (40% of military population), DMDC does not sample this group as heavily to provide sufficient responses. However, DMDC uses post-survey weighting procedures to adjust a sample with only 23% Army to make representative estimates for the Army's 40% of the overall military population. The final weighting procedures align respondent proportions back with the military population.[10]

Table 2.
Distribution of Population, Sample and Respondents, by Service

Service	Population		Sample		Respondents		Weighted Population	
	Frequency	Percent	Frequency	Percent	Frequency	Percent	Frequency	Percent
Army	544,144	40	25,010	23	4,103	18	544,144	40
Navy	312,478	23	17,956	17	3,730	16	312,478	23
Air Force	192,673	14	11,948	11	4,543	20	192,673	14
Marine Corps	323,676	24	53,564	49	10,416	46	323,676	24
Total	**1,372,971**	**100**	**108,478**	**100**	**22,792**	**100**	**1,372,971**	**100**

---

[10] *2012 WGRA* controlled for Service, gender, paygrade, and race in post-stratification weighting stage

Table 3 shows the survey subgroup breakdown by paygrade. Junior enlisted members (E1-E4) are known to have the lowest response rates. DMDC oversamples this group to provide enough responses to make representative estimates (44% of the population versus 60% of the sample). Higher responding groups such as high ranking officers or senior enlisted members are under sampled. The high response rates among these specific subgroups provide a sufficient number of respondents. The respondents DMDC received for the *2012 WGRA* are consistent with expected rates based on historical trends. Using post-stratification the final weighted population is pulled back into population alignment.

Table 3.
Distribution of Population, Sample and Respondents, by Paygrade

Paygrade	Population		Sample		Respondents		Weighted Population	
	Frequency	Percent	Frequency	Percent	Frequency	Percent	Frequency	Percent
E1-E4	600,304	44	65,401	60	8,223	36	600,304	44
E5-E9	539,086	39	29,360	27	9,116	40	539,086	39
W1-W3	19,639	1	1,426	1	631	3	19,639	1
O1-O3	126,711	9	8,417	8	2,994	13	126,711	9
O4-O6	87,231	6	3,847	4	1,828	8	87,231	6
Total	1,372,971	100	108,478	100	22,792	100	1,372,971	100

Table 4 shows the survey subgroup breakdown by gender. For the *2012 WGRA* females were significantly over sampled considering they are disproportionately victims of USC, and key estimation domains required large sample sizes from both genders. Overall females made up 42% of the sample compared to 15% of the overall active duty military population. The final weighted population pulls the respondents back into alignment with gender composition in the active duty to ensure final weighted estimates are not over-representing females.

Table 4.
Distribution of Population, Sample and Respondents, by Gender

Gender	Population		Sample		Respondents		Weighted Population	
	Frequency	Percent	Frequency	Percent	Frequency	Percent	Frequency	Percent
Male	1,173,090	85	63,177	58	11,245	49	1,173,090	85
Female	199,881	15	45,301	42	11,547	51	199,881	15
Total	1,372,971	100	108,478	100	22,792	100	1,372,971	100

Table 5 shows the survey subgroup breakdown by race/ethnicity.[11] Minority members typically have lower response rates because they are composed of more junior enlisted. Therefore DMDC sampled minority members at higher rates. Population controls adjust the population back into alignment.

Table 5.
Distribution of Population, Sample and Respondents, by Minority/Non-Minority

Race	Population		Sample		Respondents		Weighted Population	
	Frequency	Percent	Frequency	Percent	Frequency	Percent	Frequency	Percent
Non-Minority	887,500	65	63,704	59	13,653	60	887,500	65
Minority	485,471	35	44,774	41	9,139	40	485,471	35
Total	1,372,971	100	108,478	100	22,792	100	1,372,971	100

Summary of Sample Composition Compared With Survey Respondents

The WGRA sample composition demographically differs from the active duty population distribution due to intentional sampling strategies that allow precise estimation for small subgroups. The respondent composition differs from the sample distribution in predictable ways due to subgroups (e.g., junior enlisted) responding at different rates. Analyses show that the survey weights effectively eliminate these differences and the distribution of weighted survey respondents closely matches the active duty population. The difference in the composition of the respondents compared with the population distributions is effectively eliminated during survey weighting, and therefore this study provides no indication of NRB in WGRA estimates.

---

[11] Race: Non-Minority—White, Minority—Black, Hispanic, Other

Section III:
Assess How Effectively DMDC Weighting Reduces Nonresponse Bias

This component of the *2012 WGRA* NRB study was conducted in two phases. Phase 1 identified influential demographic variables, defined as variables that significantly predict whether a sample member responds to the survey. Identification of influential variables was based on both experience with military gender relations surveys and responses to the current survey. Phase 2 examined whether the influential variables identified in Phase 1 show significant differences in predicting response patterns to some important survey questions. If a demographic variable exhibits statistical significance in both phases, then potential NRB is indicated and further analysis is performed.

The terms characteristics, variables, and factors are used interchangeably throughout this report. The *2012 WGRA* return dataset was used for the study. The dataset consists of active duty members in Army, Navy, Marine Corps, and Air Force. The analysis was performed on the *2012 WGRA* complete respondents and nonrespondents consisting of 91,402 members of which 22,792 completed the survey and 68,610 nonrespondents. For this analysis, we excluded 17,076 sample members with disposition codes of postal non-deliverables, refusals, and ineligibles.

Phase 1: Modeling Survey Response

Respondents and nonrespondents are characterized based on a set of demographic variables. These characteristics were identified based on the survey response and based on DMDC's experience in military surveys. Experience shows that variables such as member's gender, paygrade, and Service are critical in predicting military survey response. Nine demographic variables based on DMDC's *April 2012 ADMF* were identified, statistically tested, and determined to have significant predictive power on the *2012 WGRA* survey response. These variables are the member's gender, Service, occupation code, education, paygrade, race/ethnicity, marital status, deployment in the last 12 months, and location. The deployment variable was based on the *April 2012 Contingency Tracking System (CTS)* for deployments in Iraq and Afghanistan (Operation Iraqi Freedom and Operation Enduring Freedom). Table 6 shows the nine variables along with their corresponding levels.

Table 6.
Independent Demographic Variables

Variable/Characteristic	Categories
Gender	Male
	Female
Service	Army
	Navy
	Marine Corps
	Air Force
Occupation Code	Combat
	Combat Support
Education	No college
	Some college
	4 year degree
	Grad/Prof degree
Paygrade	E1-E3
	E4
	E5-E6
	E7-E9
	W1-W5
	O1-O3
	O4-O6
Race/Ethnicity	White
	Black
	Hispanic
	Other
Marital Status	Not Married
	Married
Deployment	Never Deployed Since 9/11
	Not Deployed in the Past 12 Months
	Deployed in the Past 12 Months
Location	US & US territories
	Europe
	Other
	Asia & Pacific Islands

The analysis of survey response in Phase 1 consisted of two steps. First, all nine characteristics were examined individually utilizing Simple Logistic Regression. The dependent variable of the logistic model is a binary variable representing the response to the survey where the variable equals 0 for nonresponse and 1 for response. Nine logistic regression analyses were performed, one for each variable in Table 6. In other words, the response to the survey was modeled using each of the nine demographic variables one at a time. If the variable shows significant impact on predicting response to the survey then it is flagged as a potential driver of NRB and further analysis was performed.

Second, all variables with individual predictive power of survey response were tested simultaneously via a logistic regression full model. The full model is a main effect logistic model that includes all the variables exhibiting significant differences when tested individually. The purpose of testing the full model is to measure the effect of each variable controlling for the others (i.e., measuring the effect of one characteristic taking the other characteristics into consideration).

To perform statistical modeling using logistic regression, it is customary that one of the categories (levels) of the independent variable is set to be a reference category; typically either the first or the last. We modeled using the first category as a reference. All other categories of the variable were compared with the reference category and the model parameters and odds ratios were derived and interpreted accordingly. The odds ratio can be interpreted as the odds of one variable being more predictive in comparison to another. If the characteristic significantly predicts response to the survey, the odds ratios are examined to determine the source of significance. To illustrate, the process of modeling the paygrade variable is described below. The other variables are similarly modeled and interpreted.

Modeling the Paygrade Variable: The paygrade variable consists of seven categories (levels): E1-E3, E4, E5-E6, E7-E9, W1-W5, O1-O3, and O4-O6. The reference category is paygrade E1-E3. Every other paygrade category is compared to the reference category via the odds ratio. Table 7 shows the frequencies of each paygrade category along with the number of respondents and nonrespondents and the reference assignment. Notice that zeros were assigned to the reference category (E1-E3). The first comparison to the reference will be for paygrade E4, then for paygrade E5-E6, and so on.

Table 7.
Categorical Variable Coding

		Frequency	Nonresponse	Response	Parameter Coding					
					(1)	(2)	(3)	(4)	(5)	(6)
Paygrade	E1-E3	33,192	28,561	4,631	0	0	0	0	0	0
	E4	19,714	16,122	3,592	1	0	0	0	0	0
	E5-E6	20,875	14,349	6,526	0	1	0	0	0	0
	E7-E9	5,237	2,647	2,590	0	0	1	0	0	0
	W1-W5	1,297	666	631	0	0	0	1	0	0
	O1-O3	7,526	4,532	2,994	0	0	0	0	1	0
	O4-O6	3,561	1,733	1,828	0	0	0	0	0	1
Total			91,402	68,610	22,792					

The next analysis was to run a simple logistic regression model where paygrade is the independent variable and calculate the Likelihood Ratio Chi-Square test. The Likelihood Ratio Chi-Square test resulted in a value of 7,084 and p-value < .05 indicating that paygrade significantly predicts response to the survey (P-Value column, Table 8). Table 8 contains the results of significance testing for the paygrade variable and its categories. Notice that the reference category E1-E3 is not displayed since the odds ratios of the other paygrade categories are compared to the reference group and the odds ratio of the reference category to itself is 1.

Table 8.
Significance Testing of Paygrade

	P-Value	Odds Ratio	95% C.I. for Odds Ratio	
			Lower	Upper
Paygrade	0.000*			
E4	0.000*	1.374	1.310	1.441
E5-E6	0.000*	2.805	2.688	2.927
E7-E9	0.000*	6.035	5.669	6.423
W1-W5	0.000*	5.843	5.218	6.544
O1-O3	0.000*	4.074	3.854	4.307
O4-O6	0.000*	6.505	6.049	6.996
Constant	0.000*	.162		

*Indicates statistical significance at $\alpha = .05$

Because paygrade is a significant predictor of survey response, we next examined the odds ratio of each paygrade levels to determine the source of significant differences. The odds ratio (Odds Ratio column, Table 8) was calculated with respect to the reference category; it is simply the odds of one category divided by the odds of the reference category. If the odds of the two levels are the same, then one would expect the odds ratio to be close to 1.0. An odds ratio greater than 1.0 indicates the comparison, in this case paygrade level, is more likely to respond to the survey than the reference group, while an odds ratio less than 1.0 implies the opposite. Consider the paygrade E5-E6. The corresponding odds ratio is about 2.8. This means that members of paygrade E5-E6 are about three times more likely to respond to the survey than members of E1-E3, and their response is statistically different than members of paygrade E1-E3 (p-value <0.05). Similarly, E7-E9's are about six times more likely to respond to the survey (odds ratio = 6.035) and their response propensity is significantly different than E1-E3's (p-value < 0.05). Notice that within enlisted and within officers, the odds ratio increases as the rank increases indicating that senior members have a higher likelihood of responding to the survey. Moreover, not only is the overall paygrade variable significant, but all paygrade categories are statistically significant as well. The 95% confidence interval of the odds ratios is also given for further interpretation.

The other variables were similarly modeled and interpreted. All nine variables showed significant predictive power of survey response.

Since all nine characteristics differed significantly between the two groups (respondents and nonrespondents), all characteristics were then examined simultaneously to measure the impact of one variable in predicting response to the survey while controlling for the other eight variables. Logistic regression was again employed. As in the first step, the dependent variable

16

represents the response to the survey and the independent variables are the demographic variables listed in Table 9. Likelihood Ratio Chi-Square tests with p-values < 0.05 (P-Value column, Table 9) indicate significant differences in response rates. The results of significance for each variable in the model and its corresponding categories are shown in Table 9. Notice that the reference category is not displayed in the table for the reason mentioned earlier. Column 1 show the independent variables and their categories, the second through fifth columns consist of the parameter estimates (B), the standard errors of the estimate (S.E.), the Wald tests, and the degrees of freedom (df) associated with the variables and categories respectively.

All overall characteristics are still significant in the full model. The Likelihood Ratio Chi-Square for this model was 10,506.96 and the corresponding p-value was <.05 suggesting that the model fits the data (i.e., the nine independent variables used in the model are significant in predicting survey response).

Wald's test and the corresponding p-values for all independent variables at almost all levels are significant (p-value < 0.05) suggesting that these variables exhibit significant power for predicting *2012 WGRA* survey response.

The odds ratios (Odds Ratio column, Table 9) for each variable in the full model are derived taking the impact of the other variables in the model into consideration (i.e., controlling for the other variables). To illustrate the practical importance of the difference between results from this model, where all the variables are examined simultaneously, and the results in the previous step, where each variable is examined independently, consider the odds ratio of the paygrade variable in both cases. The odds ratio for paygrade E7-E9 is 6.035 (Table 8) in the bivariate model. This indicates that E7-E9 members are about six times as likely as E1-E3 (the reference group) to respond to the survey. However, in the full model the odds ratio for E7-E9, when the effect of the other demographic characteristics is taken into considerations, is lower (5.441 in Table 9). This indicates that if the impact of all the demographic variables is considered at once, E7-E9 members are 5.4 times as likely as E1-E3 to respond to the survey.

Table 9.
Full Logistic Model with Nine Independent Variables for Phase 1

	Parameter Estimate	Standard Error	Wald Test Statistic	df	P-Value	Odds Ratio	95 Percent C.I. for Odds Ratio	
							Lower	Upper
Females	.412	.018	514.243	1	0.000*	1.510	1.457	1.565
Service			1,393.260	3	0.000*			
Navy	.286	.028	107.810	1	0.000*	1.331	1.261	1.405
Marine Corps	.613	.024	667.597	1	0.000*	1.846	1.762	1.934
Air Force	.967	.028	1,183.217	1	0.000*	2.631	2.490	2.780
Combat Support	.518	.023	489.615	1	0.000*	1.679	1.603	1.758
Education			96.827	3	0.000*			
Some College	.172	.032	29.905	1	0.000*	1.188	1.117	1.264
4 Year Degree	.296	.034	76.286	1	0.000*	1.345	1.258	1.437
Grad/Pro Degree	.292	.050	33.739	1	0.000*	1.339	1.213	1.477
Paygrade			2,851.411	6	0.000*			
E4	.280	.026	114.290	1	0.000*	1.323	1.257	1.392
E5-E6	.929	.027	1,212.656	1	0.000*	2.531	2.402	2.667
E7-E9	1.694	.037	2,070.496	1	0.000*	5.441	5.058	5.853
W1-W5	1.760	.062	794.583	1	0.000*	5.815	5.145	6.572
O1-O3	1.098	.041	734.899	1	0.000*	2.999	2.770	3.247
O4-O6	1.544	.057	736.009	1	0.000*	4.682	4.188	5.234
Race/Ethnicity			133.698	3	0.000*			
Black	-.260	.024	121.546	1	0.000*	.771	.736	.807
Hispanic	-.053	.025	4.556	1	0.033*	.948	.903	.996
Other	.045	.031	2.154	1	0.142	1.046	.985	1.110
Married	.176	.018	98.301	1	0.000*	1.193	1.152	1.235
Deployment			15.712	2	0.000*			
Not Deployed Past 12 Months	-.080	.021	14.306	1	0.000*	.923	.886	.962
Deployed Past 12 Months	-.073	.028	7.033	1	0.008*	.929	.880	.981
Location			108.565	3	0.000*			
Europe	-.017	.046	.140	1	0.708	.983	.899	1.075
Other	-.311	.043	52.772	1	0.000*	.733	.674	.797
Asia & Pacific Islands	.215	.031	48.115	1	0.000*	1.240	1.167	1.318
Constant	-2.875	.034	7,262.651	1	0.000*	.056		

*Indicates statistical significance at $\alpha = .05$

Table 9 shows that after controlling for the effects of the other variables, the odds ratios for most demographic variables categories are still statistically significant and some odds ratios are substantially different from 1.0.

- Females are about 1.5 times as likely to respond to the survey as males.

18

- Senior enlisted members (E7-E9) are more than five times as likely to respond to the survey as junior enlisted members (E1-E3).

- Senior officers (O4-O6) are more than 4.5 times as likely to respond as junior enlisted.

- Members in combat support are about 1.7 times as likely to respond as members in combat category.

- Members identifying as Black are about 0.8 times as likely to respond as those identifying as White.

While the odds ratios in the full model are mostly significant and substantially different from 1.0, the overall variance accounted for by the model of nine independent variables is only 11% based on the Cox and Snell R-Square, suggesting that the size of the bias associated with survey nonresponse is minimal.

Additionally, in accordance with industry practice, the *2012 WGRA* response data were weighted to compensate for both variable sampling rates and differential survey nonresponse. Studies of NRB support that adjusting survey weights for nonresponse and poststratifying to known totals can significantly reduce NRB (Brick & Bose, 2001). The *2012 WGRA* weighting used two phases of nonresponse adjustments, followed by post-stratification to ensure weighted estimates of known demographics matched administrative counts on the frame. Seven of the nine variables that showed predictive power of nonresponse in this study; paygrade, Service, gender, race/ethnicity, marital status, deployment in the past 12 months, and occupation were used during survey weighting. The only two variables that were not used to weight the data were education and location.

To assess the impact of education and location on nonresponse (i.e., to measure the amount of bias caused by these two variables that was not accounted for through the weighting process), a separate logistic regression model was run including only these two variables as independent variables. The amount of variance accounted for by this model is relatively low, only 4%, suggesting that education and location that were not accounted for through the weighting process do not have high predictive power.

Having identified a set of variables impacting the response to the survey, next we measured the impact of these variables on survey questions. Variables exhibiting significant predictive power on survey response and on response to questions are considered drivers of potential nonresponse bias.

Phase 2: Modeling USC & Sexual Harassment

In this phase, the impact of the nine variables identified in Phase 1 to have significant predictive power on survey response were investigated in terms of their impact on the response to important survey questions. If a variable significantly predicted both the response to the survey (Phase 1) and the response to the survey questions, estimates for these questions may be at risk for NRB if not properly accounted for during weighting.

We identified 31 important questions (USC and sexual harassment) from the *2012 WGRA* survey for the Phase 2 analysis. Some of the questions were asked to all survey respondents while others are only asked based on responses to prior questions (i.e., skip patterns). Table 10 lists these questions.

We again used logistic regression models to measure the effects of the demographic variables on each question. The response to the question represents the dependent variable and the nine variables identified in Phase 1 are the predictors (independent variables).

To perform the logistic regression, we dichotomized all dependent variables by collapsing groups of similar categories together to form a binary variable with values of 0 or 1. The response with the higher number (1 in this case) is the modeled category. The original and the collapsed levels are shown in Table 10 and consists of five columns; the variable name in the database, question number in the survey, question text, response levels and the collapsed levels/categories with the assigned value of 0 or 1. To clarify, consider the reporting type variable "REPTYPE." This variable has three levels where level 1 represents "restricted report," level 2 represents "unrestricted report," and level 3 represents "restricted report that was converted to an unrestricted report." We collapsed levels 2 and 3 to form the modeled category "unrestricted reporting" taking on value of 1, and the other category "restricted reporting" taking on a value of 0.

Table 10.
Questions Reviewed for NRB and Collapsing Decisions

Variable	Question Number	Question Text	Response Levels	Collapsed/ Recoded for Modeling
USCRATE	32	In the past 12 months, have you experienced any of the following intentional sexual contacts that were against your will or occurred when you did not or could not consent where someone... Sexually touched you (e.g., intentional touching of genitalia, breasts, or buttocks) or made you sexually touch them? Attempted to make you have sexual intercourse, but was not successful? Made you have sexual intercourse? Attempted to make you perform or receive oral sex, anal sex, or penetration by a finger or object, but was not successful? Made you perform or receive oral sex, anal sex, or penetration by a finger or object?	1 No / 2 Yes	0 No / 1 Yes
SEXHAR	Constructed from Q30a, c, e-f, h, j-p, and Q31	Sexual Harassment Incident Rate: Sexual Harassment can be defined as experiences of Crude/Offensive Behavior, Unwanted Sexual Attention, or Sexual Coercion.	1 Did not experience / 2 Experienced	0 Did not experience / 1 Experienced

Table 10. (continued)

Variable	Question Number	Question Text	Response Levels	Collapsed/ Recoded for Modeling
PTSD	Construct	Posttraumatic Stress Disorder (PTSD) score: Constructed from Q23. PTSD is a type of trauma and stress-related disorder that can be triggered by experiencing or witnessing a traumatic event that causes fear, helplessness, or horror and is characterized by persistent frightening thoughts and memories, emotional detachment or numbness, sleep problems, and a tendency to be easily startled. The scale ranges from 17 to 85. A score of 50 or higher on the PTSD Checklist is considered indicative of probable PTSD diagnosis.	Scale 17-49 does not indicate PTSD	0 for scale 17-49
			Scale 50 and above indicates PTSD	1 for scale 50-85
DRGALCR	Constructed from Q39-Q41	Use of alcohol or drugs in this situation.	1 No	0 No
			2 Yes	1 Yes
SAREPCIV	45	Did you report this situation to a civilian authority or organization?	1 No	0 No
			2 Yes	1 Yes
SAREPMIL	46	Did you report this situation to an installation/Service/DoD authority or organization?	1 No	0 No
			2 Yes	1 Yes
REPTYPE	47	Did you make...	1 Only a restricted report?	0 Only a restricted report?
			2 Only an unrestricted report?	1 Only an unrestricted report?
			3 A restricted report that was converted to an unrestricted report?	1 A restricted report that was converted to an unrestricted report?
SAONESITA	34a	What did the person(s) do during the situation? Sexually touched you (e.g., intentional touching of genitalia, breasts, or buttocks) or made you sexually touch them	1 Did not do this	0 Did not do this
			2 Did this	1 Did this
SAONESITB	34b	What did the person(s) do during the situation? Attempted to make you have sexual intercourse, but was not successful	1 Did not do this	0 Did not do this
			2 Did this	1 Did this
SAONESITC	34c	What did the person(s) do during the situation? Made you have sexual intercourse	1 Did not do this	0 Did not do this
			2 Did this	1 Did this
SAONESITD	34d	What did the person(s) do during the situation? Attempted to make you perform or receive oral sex, anal sex, or penetration by a finger or object, but was not successful	1 Did not do this	0 Did not do this
			2 Did this	1 Did this

Table 10. (continued)

Variable	Question Number	Question Text	Response Levels	Collapsed/ Recoded for Modeling
SAONESITE	34e	What did the person(s) do during the situation? Made you perform or receive oral sex, anal sex, or penetration by a finger or object	1 Did not do this	0 Did not do this
			2 Did this	1 Did this
SAOCCURA	35a	Did the situation occur... At a military installation?	1 No	0 No
			2 Yes	1 Yes
SAOCCURB	35b	Did the situation occur... During your work day/duty hours?	1 No	0 No
			2 Yes	1 Yes
SAOCCURC	35c	Did the situation occur... While you were on TDY/TAD, at sea, or during field exercises/alerts?	1 No	0 No
			2 Yes	1 Yes
SAOCCURD	35d	Did the situation occur... While you were deployed to a combat zone or to an area where you drew imminent danger pay or hostile fire pay?	1 No	0 No
			2 Yes	1 Yes
SAOCCURE	35e	Did the situation occur... During the delayed entry program?	1 No	0 No
			2 Yes	1 Yes
SAOCCURF	35f	Did the situation occur... During recruit training/basic training?	1 No	0 No
			2 Yes	1 Yes
SAOCCURG	35g	Did the situation occur... During any type of military combat training?	1 No	0 No
			2 Yes	1 Yes
SAOCCURH	35h	Did the situation occur... During Officer Candidate or Training School/Basic or Advanced Officer Course?	1 No	0 No
			2 Yes	1 Yes
SAOCCURI	35i	Did the situation occur... During military occupational specialty school/technical training/advanced individual training/professional military education?	1 No	0 No
			2 Yes	1 Yes
SAOFFENDA	38a	Was the offender(s)... Someone in your chain of command?	1 No	0 No
			2 Yes	1 Yes
SAOFFENDB	38b	Was the offender(s)... Other military person(s) of higher rank/grade who was not in your chain of command?	1 No	0 No
			2 Yes	1 Yes

Table 10. (continued)

Variable	Question Number	Question Text	Response Levels	Collapsed/ Recoded for Modeling
SAOFFENDC	38c	Was the offender(s)... Your military coworker(s)?	1 No	0 No
			2 Yes	1 Yes
SAOFFENDD	38d	Was the offender(s)... Your military subordinate(s)?	1 No	0 No
			2 Yes	1 Yes
SAOFFENDE	38e	Was the offender(s)... Other military person(s)?	1 No	0 No
			2 Yes	1 Yes
SAOFFENDF	38f	Was the offender(s)... DoD/Service civilian employee(s)?	1 No	0 No
			2 Yes	1 Yes
SAOFFENDG	38g	Was the offender(s)... DoD/Service civilian contractor(s)?	1 No	0 No
			2 Yes	1 Yes
SAOFFENDJ	38h	Was the offender(s)... Your spouse/significant other?	1 No	0 No
			2 Yes	1 Yes
SAOFFENDH	38i	Was the offender(s)... Person(s) in the local community	1 No	0 No
			2 Yes	1 Yes
SAOFFENDI	38j	Was the offender(s)... Unknown person(s)?	1 No	0 No
			2 Yes	1 Yes

For each of the variables listed in Table 10, logistic regression analysis was performed to determine whether the variables that predicted response to the survey (Phase 1) also predict the response pattern to the questions. Each model included all nine variables that were significant in predicting survey response from Phase 1. If the overall model fits the data (i.e., if the Likelihood Ratio Chi-Square test is significant [p-value <.05]) this indicates that at least one of the characteristics is significant in predicting response to the questions. Accordingly, further investigation of the odds ratio is performed to determine which characteristics are significant (i.e., to determine which variables are potential drivers of NRB).

Table 11 shows the significance testing results along with the most influential variables for each model, as well as the total number of respondents and number of respondents by category. Twenty-three of the 31 models were statistically significant (p-value < 0.05) Conclusions (i.e., significance) for some variables where the modeled category is less than 100 may not be statistically supportable since the size of the modeled category may be too small to model (e.g., the size of the modeled category in the variable SAOCCURH is only 41).

Significant fit of the model to the data indicates that at least one of the variables in the model significantly predicts responses to the question. For example, the USCRATE model with nine predictors fits the data, meaning at least one of the nine variables is significant in predicting the response pattern to the USC question. For this model, six of the nine variables were significant (gender, Service, education, paygrade, race/ethnicity, and marital status). Because these six variables are significant in both phases we can say that the estimates derived from this question exhibit potential NRB. Different sets of variables have predictive power in different models (i.e., for different survey questions). In some cases only one of the nine independent variables appears to have significant predictive power on the response to questions.

Some variables are significant in more models than others:

- Gender appeared in 21 of the 23 significant models.

- Service appeared in eight models.

- Paygrade, race/ethnicity, marital status, and deployment appeared in six models.

- Education in two models.

- Location and occupation code each appeared in only one model.

Table 11.
Logistic Models for the 31 Questions in Phase 2

Variable	Question Text	Total Number of Respondents	Likelihood Ratio Chi-Square Test	P-Value	Variables With Significant Predictive Value
USCRATE	In the past 12 months, have you experienced any of the following intentional sexual contacts that were against your will or occurred when you did not or could not consent where someone... Sexually touched you (e.g., intentional touching of genitalia, breasts, or buttocks) or made you sexually touch them? Attempted to make you have sexual intercourse, but was not successful? Made you have sexual intercourse? Attempted to make you perform or receive oral sex, anal sex, or penetration by a finger or object, but was not successful? Made you perform or receive oral sex, anal sex, or penetration by a finger or object?	Total = 22,792 No = 21,960 Yes = 832	889.73	0.000*	Gender Service Education Paygrade Race/Ethnicity Marital Status

*Indicates statistical significance at $\alpha = .05$

24

Table 11. (continued)

Variable	Question Text	Total Number of Respondents	Likelihood Ratio Chi-Square Test	P-Value	Variables With Significant Predictive Value
SEXHAR	Sexual Harassment incident rate: Constructed from Q30a, c, e-f, h, j-p, and Q31. Sexual Harassment can be defined as experiences of Crude/Offensive Behavior, Unwanted Sexual Attention, or Sexual Coercion.	Total = 22,792 Did not experience = 19,728 Experienced = 3,064	2,974.26	0.000*	Gender Service Paygrade Race/Ethnicity Marital Status Deployment
PTSD	Posttraumatic Stress Disorder (PTSD) score: Constructed from Q23. PTSD is a type of trauma and stress-related disorder that can be triggered by experiencing or witnessing a traumatic event that causes fear, helplessness, or horror and is characterized by persistent frightening thoughts and memories, emotional detachment or numbness, sleep problems, and a tendency to be easily startled. The scale ranges from 17 to 85. A score of 50 or higher on the PTSD Checklist is considered indicative of probable PTSD diagnosis.	Total = 22,488 Not PTSD = 20,068 2PTSD = 2,420	777.96	0.000*	Gender Service Education Paygrade Race/Ethnicity Deployment
SAONESITA	Sexually touched you (e.g., intentional touching of genitalia, breasts, or buttocks) or made you sexually touch them	Total = 807 Did not do this = 181 Did this = 626	62.94	0.000*	Gender
SAONESITB	Attempted to make you have sexual intercourse, but was not successful	Total = 792 Did not do this = 497 Did this = 295	72.91	0.000*	Gender
SAONESITC	Made you have sexual intercourse	Total = 798 Did not do this = 607 Did this = 191	58.65	0.000*	Gender Deployment
SAONESITD	Attempted to make you perform or receive oral sex, anal sex, or penetration by a finger or object, but was not successful	Total = 798 Did not do this = 595 Did this = 203	46.98	0.002*	Gender
SAONESITE	Made you perform or receive oral sex, anal sex, or penetration by a finger or object	Total = 799 Did not do this = 656 Did this = 143	59.36	0.000*	Gender Race/Ethnicity
SAOCCURA	Did the situation occur... At a military installation?	Total = 800 No = 275 Yes = 525	88.70	0.000*	Service Paygrade

*Indicates statistical significance at α= .05

Table 11. (continued)

Variable	Question Text	Total Number of Respondents	Likelihood Ratio Chi-Square Test	P-Value	Variables With Significant Predictive Value
SAOCCURB	Did the situation occur... During your work day/duty hours?	Total = 803 No = 502 Yes = 301	95.86	0.000*	Gender Service Paygrade Marital Status Deployment
SAOCCURC	Did the situation occur... While you were on TDY/TAD, at sea, or during field exercises/alerts?	Total = 796 No = 612 Yes = 184	69.52	0.000*	Paygrade Marital Status Deployment
SAOCCURD	Did the situation occur... While you were deployed to a combat zone or to an area where you drew imminent danger pay or hostile fire pay?	Total = 802 No = 658 Yes = 144	143.56	0.000*	Gender Deployment Location
SAOCCURE	Did the situation occur... During the delayed entry program?	Total = 803 No = 750 Yes = 53	43.69	0.006*	Gender
SAOCCURF	Did the situation occur... During recruit training/basic training?	Total = 800 No = 754 Yes = 46	46.04	0.003*	Gender Service
SAOCCURG	Did the situation occur... During any type of military combat training?	Total = 801 No = 724 Yes = 77	50.19	0.001*	Gender Service
SAOCCURH	Did the situation occur... During Officer Candidate or Training School/Basic or Advanced Officer Course?	Total = 798 No = 757 Yes = 41	49.67	0.001*	Gender
SAOCCURI	Did the situation occur... During military occupational specialty school/technical training/advanced individual training/professional military education?	Total = 797 No = 658 Yes = 139	46.87	0.002*	Gender Occupation Code
SAOFFENDA	Was the offender(s)... Someone in your chain of command?	Total = 783 No = 568 Yes = 215	33.74	0.069	Model is not significant but Service is
SAOFFENDB	Was the offender(s)... Other military person(s) of higher rank/grade who was not in your chain of command?	Total = 782 No = 504 Yes = 278	18.30	0.608	None
SAOFFENDC	Was the offender(s)... Your military coworker(s)?	Total = 780 No = 356 Yes = 424	16.26	0.844	None
SAOFFENDD	Was the offender(s)... Your military subordinate(s)?	Total = 777 No = 651 Yes = 126	45.62	0.003*	Gender

*Indicates statistical significance at α= .05

26

Table 11. (continued)

Variable	Question Text	Total Number of Respondents	Likelihood Ratio Chi-Square Test	P-Value	Variables With Significant Predictive Value
SAOFFENDE	Was the offender(s)... Other military person(s)?	Total = 778 No = 478 Yes = 300	30.42	0.138	None
SAOFFENDF	Was the offender(s)... DoD/Service civilian employee(s)?	Total = 778 No = 725 Yes = 53	65.87	0.000*	Gender
SAOFFENDG	Was the offender(s)... DoD/Service civilian contractor(s)?	Total = 779 No = 734 Yes = 45	52.95	0.000*	Gender
SAOFFENDH	Was the offender(s)... Person(s) in the local community?	Total = 781 No = 711 Yes = 70	24.99	0.351	Model is not significant but gender is
SAOFFENDI	Was the offender(s)... Unknown person(s)?	Total = 776 No = 688 Yes = 88	27.87	0.221	Model is not significant but gender is
SAOFFENDJ	Was the offender(s)... Your spouse/significant other?	Total = 783 No = 714 Yes = 69	50.39	0.001*	Gender Marital Status
DRGALCR	Use of alcohol or drugs in this situation. Constructed from Q39-Q41	Total = 782 No = 380 Yes = 402	103.10	0.000*	Gender Service Race/Ethnicity Marital Status
SAREPCIV	Did you report this situation to a civilian authority or organization?	Total = 775 No = 658 Yes = 117	29.37	0.169	None
SAREPMIL	Did you report this situation to an installation/Service/DoD authority or organization?	Total = 774 No = 544 Yes = 230	48.36	0.002*	Gender Race/Ethnicity
REPTYPE	Did you make... *Mark one.*	Total = 225 Restricted Reporting = 59 Unrestricted Reporting = 166	26.95	0.258	None

*Indicates statistical significance at α= .05

In conclusion, all nine predictors of survey response in Phase 1 are also significant in one way or another in Phase 2, suggesting that the nine characteristics (gender, Service, paygrade, location, occupation code, gender, marital status, education, and deployment in the last 12 months) are indicative of potential NRB. However, as mentioned above, the *2012 WGRA* response data were weighted using seven of the nine variables that showed predictive power of nonresponse in this study (all except education and location). Therefore, omitting education and location from weighting had a minimal impact on final weighted estimates.

We investigated the impact of education and location for every model where education, location, or both had significant predictive value (appeared in the last column of Table 11). Education had significant predictive power in two models (USCRATE and PTSD). Location had significant predictive power in SAOCCURD. Accordingly, two logistic regression analyses consisting of education as the only independent variable in the model, and one analysis consisting of location as the only independent variable in the model were performed to assess the impact of the education variable or location variable on responses to the questions. In the two questions where education appeared to be a significant predictor, the variance accounted for by education was only 2% of the variance of survey estimates for USC and approximately 2.6% for PTSD. In the one question where location was significant, the variance accounted for by location was only 0.4% of the variance in survey estimates. This suggests that the variance not accounted for due to education and location is relatively low and hence the bias associated with survey nonresponse is likely small. While their impact looks minor, DMDC will consider the addition of both these variables to the weighting process for future WGRA surveys.

DMDC performed additional analyses by comparing the Likelihood Ratio Chi-Square statistic for the full model against the reduced model that omits education and location. Similar conclusions were reached indicating minimal impact of these variables on NRB.

Summary of Assessment on How Effectively DMDC Weighting Reduces Nonresponse Bias

To indirectly estimate the impact of nonresponse on survey results for the *2012 WGRA*, a two-phase study was conducted.

In Phase 1, nine demographic variables were identified as having potential NRB impact on survey results. DMDC's experience with military surveys coupled with the responses of the *2012 WGRA* suggested these variables are critical in predicting survey response. Analyses in Phase 1 showed that the nine identified variables have a substantial, statistically significant impact on a member's likelihood to respond to the survey.

Further investigation in Phase 2 indicated that these nine characteristics are significant predictors of response patterns to survey questions. Statistical significance of the nine variables in both phases of the analysis indicated potential NRB in the *2012 WGRA* survey estimates.

However, seven of the nine characteristics were accounted for during *2012 WGRA* weighting, including nonresponse and post-stratification adjustments, so contribution of these variables to NRB is of little concern since such adjustments can significantly reduce that bias (Brick and Bose, 2001).

Further analysis of the two variables not included in the weighting process, education and location, indicated that the variables accounted for relatively small variance in survey estimates ranging from 0.4% to 2.6%. Therefore, while NRB is not eliminated, its effect is relatively small.

Section IV:
Use of Late Respondents as Proxy for Nonrespondents

Survey researchers have observed that if the field period were shortened or fewer contact attempts were used, a subset of survey respondents would have been nonrespondents, and they have hypothesized that these late respondents may be more similar to nonrespondents than the early respondents. This hypothesis is called the "continuum of resistance" model (Lin & Schaeffer, 1995). Although results from studies testing this model have been mixed (Groves & Peytcheva, 2008); analysis of late respondents is still a common practice in NRB studies.

DMDC evaluated whether early and late respondents to the *2012 WGRA* survey reported different USC rates, and whether differences in USC rates were potentially caused by observable characteristics (e.g., gender, race) adjusted for during weighting. Because differences in USC rates between early and late respondents could be explained by demographics (e.g., junior enlisted disproportionately respond late), we conducted this analysis 1) unweighted and 2) weighted by a new set of weights specific to this analysis (late weights). The late weights separately weight the early respondents and late respondents to the full active duty population as if they were the only respondents to the survey. In other words, these weights remove the effects of underlying demographic composition and make differences between the two subgroups related only to being an early versus late respondent.

To define early and late respondents, we divided the eight week field period into two parts, treating respondents from the first six weeks as early respondents and the final two weeks as late respondents.[12] Table 12 shows the demographic composition for early respondents, late respondents, and nonrespondents by gender, Service, and paygrade.

---

[12] The choice for breaking the field period into early and late respondents is subjective. We chose the final two weeks to coincide with the final survey contact and to ensure there were sufficient numbers of late respondents to make separate estimates with reasonable precision.

Table 12.

Composition of Sample for Early, Late, and Nonrespondents

Key Domains	Early Respondents		Late Respondents		Nonrespondents	
	Number of Respondents	Unweighted Percent of Total Respondents[b]	Number of Respondents	Unweighted Percent of Total Respondents[b]	Number of Nonrespondents	Unweighted Percent of Total Nonrespondents[b]
Gender						
Male	10,111	49	1,134	50	48,981	61
Female	10,432	51	1,115	50	30,916	39
Total	**20,543**	**100**	**2,249**	**100**	**79,897**	**100**
Service						
Army	3,646	18	457	20	19,770	25
Navy	3,379	16	351	16	13,407	17
Marine Corps	9,329	45	1,087	48	40,103	50
Air Force	4,189	20	354	16	6,617	8
Total	**20,543**	**100**	**2,249**	**100**	**79,897**	**100**
Paygrade[a]						
E1-E4	7,197	35	1,026	46	53,921	67
E5-E9	8,360	41	756	34	18,432	23
O1-O3	2,695	13	299	13	4,957	6
O4-O6	1,698	8	130	6	1,863	2
Total	**20,543**	**100**	**2,249**	**100**	**79,897**	**100**

[a]We removed warrant officers from this analysis because their small numbers created small cells when creating late weights.
[b]Details may not add to totals because of rounding.

Early and late respondents generally look demographically similar; however, late respondents contain a lower percentage of Air Force (16% versus 20%) and a higher percentage of E1-E4 (46% versus 35%). WGRA late respondents are more demographically similar to the nonrespondents than the early respondents, but they are still demographically different from the nonrespondents. For instance, late respondents are disproportionately E1-E4 relative to early respondents, but nonrespondents are much more E1-E4 than late respondents (67% compared with 46%). The pattern follows for Service, where late respondents are more Army and Marine Corps, and then the effect is more pronounced for nonrespondents (e.g., 25% Army for nonrespondents versus 20% for late respondents). For gender, nonrespondents are more male and look very different from both early and late respondents. While the analysis of the demographics shows that late respondents do look more like nonrespondents, which provides limited support for the continuum of resistance model, early, late, and nonrespondents are still quite different from one another. Next, we compare USC rates for early and late respondents.

Table 13 shows that late respondents had a slightly higher unweighted USC rate (3.9% versus 3.6%), but this is not the most appropriate comparison because early and late respondents have different demographic compositions. DMDC's hypothesis was that this difference would be removed through weighting because late respondents have disproportionate representation in high-USC groups.[13] The production weights controlled for many demographic characteristics, including Service, paygrade, and gender; however, they do not control for early versus late respondents. Therefore, we created a new set of weights (late weights) to separately weight early and late respondents as if they were the only respondents to the survey. We weighted both the 20,543 early and 2,249 late respondents to the full active duty population. To create the late weights, we separately post-stratified the production WGRA final weights for early and late respondents to known administrative variable totals within post-strata defined by Service, gender, and paygrade. If necessary, we collapsed paygrade to maintain post-strata with five or more respondents. The late weights allow direct comparison of early and late respondents, and any differences will be due to unobservable differences (i.e., early respondents are more ambitious than late respondents) between the groups, and not due to differences in their demographics.

Table 13.

Comparison of Early and Late Respondents by Gender (Unweighted Versus Late Weights)

Time Period	Gender	Respondents	USC Cases	USC Rate–Unweighted (Percent)	USC Rate–Late Weights	
					Percent	Margin of Error
Early Respondents	Male	10,111	106	1.0	1.3	0.4
	Female	10,432	638	6.1	5.9	0.6
	Total	**20,543**	**744**	**3.6**	**1.9**	**0.3**
Late Respondents	Male	1,134	11	1.0	0.8	1.6
	Female	1,115	77	6.9	6.6	2.0
	Total	**2,249**	**88**	**3.9**	**1.7**	**1.1**

The table shows that when comparing early and late respondents (using late weights), late respondents have lower USC rates (1.7% compared with 1.9%), although the direction differs by gender. For females the estimated USC rate for late responders was higher (6.6% compared to 5.9%) and for males it was lower (0.8% compared to 1.3%). None of the comparisons were statistically significant (margins of error are large for late respondents). This provides limited evidence that early and late respondents have 'similar' USC rates. Therefore, if late respondents 'look like' nonrespondents, as theorized by the continuum of resistance model, this analysis provides little evidence of NRB.

A final analysis was performed using weighted logistic regression models (PROC SURVEYLOGISTIC) to determine whether the late respondents were significant in predicting USC. For this analysis the dependent variable was USC (0-did not occur and 1-occurred) and the nine independent variables were Service, gender, paygrade, occupation group (combat/non-

---

[13] That is, less likely to be Air Force who typically have lower USC rates and more likely to be E1-E4's who typically have higher USC rates, particularly among active duty women.

combat), education, race/ethnicity, marital status, deployment, location and a dummy variable for early/late respondent. A full model was run with all independent variables and a limited model was run with only the late respondent variable as the only independent variable. Similar to prior models, gender, paygrade, Service, and marital status were significant in predicting USC, but the late respondent variable was not significant in the full model (p-value=.7275) or the limited model (p-value=.9863).

Summary of Using Late Respondents as Proxy for Nonrespondents

The analysis of late respondents provides no consistent evidence of NRB in the estimates of the USC rate. Similar to nonrespondents, late respondents are disproportionately low response rate groups and groups that have higher USC rates, and therefore, as expected, late respondents have higher unweighted USC (3.9% versus 3.6%). However, this does not occur for males (1.0% for early and late respondents), and may provide evidence that nonrespondents have lower USC rates if late respondents are good proxies for nonrespondents; this is mildly supported by the demographics of late respondents (e.g., disproportionately E1-E4). After separately reweighting early and late respondents (late weights from Table 13), the late respondents have slightly lower USC rates (1.7% versus 1.9%), although the difference is small, not statistically significant, and the direction differs by gender. While the analysis of late respondents provides little evidence of NRB, we recommend cautious interpretation of these results because of the large margins of error associated with the late-weight estimates.

Section V:
Use Hard-To-Reach (HTR) Respondents as Proxy for Nonrespondents

The next analysis is similar but uses HTR respondents as proxies for nonrespondents. Similar to the late respondents it draws on the 'continuum of resistance' to use a subset of respondents to serve as a proxy for nonrespondents. The continuum of resistance suggests that the sampled members can be ordered across a continuum by the amount of difficulty needed to contact a member in order to get a completed survey. Those requiring the most effort to reach should be more similar to nonrespondents (Groves, 2006). During the *2012 WGRA* there were a total of 12 planned[14] survey contacts, including postal and e-mail announcements and reminders. For this analysis, we designated members as HTR if they had one or more of the following: 1) at least one postal non-deliverable, 2) did not have an e-mail address on file, or 3) did not have a postal address on file.

Similar to the late respondent analysis, DMDC evaluated whether HTR and regular respondents to the *2012 WGRA* survey reported different USC rates, and whether any differences were potentially caused by differences in demographic composition (e.g., gender, race). Because differences in USC rates between HTR and regular respondents could be explained by demographics (e.g., Marine Corps does not always assign e-mail addresses to junior enlisted), we conducted this analysis, 1) unweighted and 2) weighted by a new set of weights specific to this analysis (HTR weights). Similar to the late respondent analysis, HTR respondents and regular respondents were weighted separately to the full active duty population which removes the effects of underlying demographic composition and makes differences between the two subgroups related only to HTR versus regular respondent.

Table 14 compares sample sizes for regular and HTR members broken out by key demographics. The analysis does not include the 1,732 sampled members that were determined to be record ineligible[15] when the survey fielded.

---

[14] Respondents could receive additional contacts if we obtained a different postal or e-mail address after a failed contact attempt (e.g., postal non-deliverable).
[15] Most record ineligible cases have exited the military prior to fielding the survey.

Table 14.

Comparison of Sample for Regular/HTR Members by Key Demographics

Key Domains	Regular Members		HTR Members		Difference in Percentages
	Sample Size	Unweighted Percent of Total Sample	Sample Size	Unweighted Percent of Total Sample	
Gender					
Male	46,095	57	15,983	61	-4
Female	34,418	43	10,250	39	4
Total	**80,513**	**100**	**26,233**	**100**	
Service					
Army	17,945	22	6,723	26	-3
Navy	13,728	17	4,003	15	2
Marine Corps	38,366	48	14,137	54	-6
Air Force	10,474	13	1,370	5	8
Total	**80,513**	**100**	**26,233**	**100**	
Paygrade					
E1-E4	42,931	53	21,181	81	-27
E5-E9	25,416	32	3,607	14	18
W1-W5	1,285	2	127	0	1
O1-O3	7,261	9	1,094	4	5
O4-O6	3,620	5	224	1	4
Total	**80,513**	**100**	**26,233**	**100**	

HTR members are disproportionately E1-E4 (81% versus 53%), Marine Corps (54% versus 48%), and male (61% versus 57%). Some of these effects are explained because the Marine Corps does not assign email addresses to all junior enlisted and has the highest proportion of males. Junior enlisted may also move more often causing larger postal non-deliverable rates (i.e., failed postal contact attempts). Not surprisingly, high responding subgroups (E5-E9, O4-O6) make up a smaller fraction of the HTR.

Table 15 compares the demographic distributions for the regular respondents, HTR respondents, and survey nonrespondents.

Table 15.

Comparison of Respondents for Regular/HTR Members by Key Demographics

Key Domains	Regular Members		HTR Members		Nonrespondents	
	Sample Size	Unweighted Percent of Total Sample	Sample Size	Unweighted Percent of Total Sample	Sample Size	Unweighted Percent of Total Sample
Gender						
Male	10,051	49	1,194	49	48,981	61
Female	10,299	51	1,248	51	30,916	39
Total	**20,350**	**100**	**2,442**	**100**	**79,897**	**100**
Service						
Army	3,639	18	464	19	19,770	25
Navy	3,387	17	343	14	13,407	17
Marine Corps	9,086	45	1,330	54	40,103	50
Air Force	4,238	21	305	12	6,617	8
Total	**20,350**	**100**	**2,442**	**100**	**79,897**	**100**
Paygroup						
E1-E4	6,688	33	1,535	63	53,921	67
E5-E9	8,529	42	587	24	18,432	23
W1-W5	591	3	40	2	724	1
O1-O3	2,775	14	219	9	4,957	6
O4-O6	1,767	9	61	3	1,863	2
Total	**20,350**	**100**	**2,442**	**100**	**79,897**	**100**

HTR respondents tend to look like nonrespondents, including disproportionately E1-E4 (63% versus 67%) and Marine Corps (54% versus 50%). The largest differences are in the subgroups with higher USC rates.

Table 16 compares unweighted and HTR-weighted USC rates by difficulty in reaching sampled members (responder type) and gender (rows).

Table 16.

Comparison of HTR Respondents by Gender (Unweighted Versus HTR Weights)

Responder Type	Gender	Respondents	USC Cases	USC Rate– Unweighted (Percent)	USC Rate–HTR Weights	
					(Percent)	Margin of Error
Regular	Male	10,051	100	1.0	1.3	0.5
	Female	10,299	616	6.0	5.9	0.6
	Total	20,350	716	3.5	1.9	0.4
HTR	Male	1,194	17	1.4	1.1	1.2
	Female	1,248	99	7.9	7.0	1.9
	Total	**2,442**	**116**	**4.8**	**1.9**	**0.9**

As expected, HTR respondents had a higher unweighted USC rate overall (4.8% versus 3.5%), by male (1.4% versus 1.0%) and by female (7.9% versus 6.0%). DMDC's hypothesis was that this difference would likely be removed through weighting because HTR respondents may have higher USC rates simply because of their demographic composition (e.g., E1-E4 and Marine Corps have higher USC rates).

Similar to late respondent weights, HTR weights were created separately to represent the full active duty population. The late responders section contains a more detailed description of the post-stratification and adjustments to the final weights. Comparing the separately weighted USC rates we see slightly lower estimated rates for HTR males (1.1% versus 1.3%), higher USC rates for HTR females (7.0% versus 5.9%) and the same estimated rates for HTR overall (1.9%). None of the differences were statistically significant.

A final analysis was performed using weighted logistic regression models (PROC SURVEYLOGISTIC) to determine whether the HTR were significant in predicting USC. For this analysis the dependent variable was USC (0-did not occur and 1-occurred) and the nine independent variables were Service, gender, paygrade, occupation group (combat/non-combat), education, race/ethnicity, marital status, deployment, location, and a dummy variable for HTR. A full model was run with all independent variables and a limited model was run with only the HTR variable as the only independent variable. The same variables were significant in predicting USC (gender, paygrade, Service, marital status) but the HTR variable was not significant in the full model (p-value=.3755) or the limited model (p-value=.4228).

Summary of Using HTR Respondents as Proxy for Nonrespondents

Similar to late respondents, HTR sampled members are disproportionately low responding, high USC groups (E1-E4, Marine Corps). Because E1-E4 and Marine Corps have higher USC rates, we expected unweighted USC rates to be higher for HTR respondents. The analysis confirmed this expectation.

However, after separately reweighting HTR and regular respondents, HTR and regular respondents have the same USC rates (differences by gender are inconsistent and have high margins of error). Because differences between HTR and regular respondent USC rates were explained by demographics that are controlled for during WGRA production weighting, we conclude that the analysis of HTR respondents provides no evidence of NRB in WGRA production USC estimates.

Section VI:
Analyze Item Missing Data for USC Question

In this section, we analyze item missing data for the USC question to investigate the hypothesis that some respondents refuse to answer the USC question or quit the survey all together (i.e., drop-off) because of its personal and sensitive nature. If the decision to refuse to answer the question is not random (i.e., those who avoid the USC question have different USC rates than complete respondents), then a source of NRB exists. We cannot directly test this hypothesis because the USC status for respondents that avoid the question is unknown; however, we examine item missing data to assess the NRB in the USC question.

Table 17 shows the distribution of the 108,478 *2012 WGRA* sample members for the USC question. Most sampled members fail to respond to the survey (80,749); this is typical of military surveys and these unit nonrespondents provide no information for this analysis. In addition, 224 members reported being ineligible to complete the survey (left the active duty military, Q1). After removing the 22,804 members that responded to the USC question, the table shows that 4,701 respondents in the *2012 WGRA* survey did not respond to the USC question, primarily because they refused the survey, returned it blank, or quit the survey prior to completion (labeled 'Partial Respondents').

Of the 4,701 members who did not answer the USC question, 77 actively refused the survey and 873 returned a blank survey. DMDC keeps data on the reasons for active refusals and inspection of the data revealed no responses in which the member indicated he or she refused because of question content. Blank surveys are surveys that are opened and returned with no answers; respondent's motives for failing to start the survey (and therefore answer the USC question) are unknown, but we suspect some respondents have learned they can avoid future email follow-ups by submitting a blank survey.

Of the remaining nonrespondents to the USC question, 3 were ineligible and 3,748 were partial survey respondents. Partial respondents are members who started the survey but failed one or both of two criteria necessary to be used in production estimates as follows: 1) member answered less than 50% of the survey questions that are presented to all members, or 2) member failed to answer the USC question.[16] We wanted to understand whether respondents specifically avoided the USC question, or whether they quit the survey prior to ever seeing the USC question. To aid in this understanding, DMDC conducted a drop-off analysis.

---

[16] The USC question is the central question on the WGRA survey and the survey return is considered unusable without response to this question.

Table 17.
Breakdown of Sample Cases[17] to Assess Item Missing Data for the USC Question

Label	Frequency[d]		Running Subtotal
Total Sample Size	108,478		
Survey nonrespondent	- 80,749		27,729
Survey Self-Report Ineligible	- 224		27,505
Answered USC question[c]	- 22,804		4,701
Answered 'No' to USC question		21,972	
Answered 'Yes' to USC question		832	
No response (item missing for USC question)[a]	- 4,701		
Refused		- 77	4,624
Returned blank survey		- 873	3,751
Self/Proxy-report Ineligibles—deceased, ill		- 3	3,748
Partial Respondents		3,748[b]	
Dropped out at or before Q29 (likely did not see USC question [Q32])		- 3,603	145
Answered Q30/Q31 and stopped		- 88	57
Presumed active refusals (likely read USC question and did not answer)			43
Presumed passive refusals (likely did not see USC question)			45
Active refusals (skipped USC question and dropped out later)		57	0

[a]Ineligibles, Partial Respondents, Refused/deployed, and those who returned blank surveys make up the 4,701 "No Responses."
[b]The statistical methodology report shows 3,759 'partial respondents.' Those map to the 3,748 shown above and 11 that answered the USC question (all answer 'no').
[c]One Ineligible and 11 partial respondents along with the 22,792 complete respondents which makes up the 22,804 "Answered USC question."
[d]Indented frequencies sum to the row above and left.

Drop-off analysis details where survey respondents last answered an item. For example, if a respondent answered Q1-10 and quit, the drop-off analysis would place that respondent in the frequency count at Q10 (Frequency column in Table B-1). Drop-off analysis ignores skipping of questions and looks for the last question completed by the respondent. For instance, if a member answered Q1-10, skipped to 12 and answered Q12-20, and then answered no further questions, the drop-off analysis would include him/her in the count where Q20 was the last answered.

To understand whether respondents actively refused the USC question (Q32), we examined when respondents permanently stopped answering items in the survey. The question by question results of the drop-off analysis are presented in Table B-1 (Appendix B). Table B-1 shows that of the 3,748 partial respondents, 3,603 respondents dropped out of the survey either after answering Q29 or sometime before that point. Of the 145 people that remain, 88 people then answered either Q30 or Q30 and 31 (depending upon the skip pattern, respondents would have seen one or both of these questions) and then dropped out of the survey before answering

---

[17] The numbers in Table 17 do not exactly match the survey disposition codes in DMDC (2012b) because of the hierarchical assignment of disposition codes, and because Table B-1 uses the special missing codes specific to Q32.

Q32. We can further break down that group into two subgroups: presumed active refusals of Q32 (43 respondents) and presumed passive refusals of Q32 (45 respondents).

Presumed active refusals are those respondents whose last answered question was Q30 and because of their answers would have been advanced to Q32. In order for the data from Q30 to have been submitted to the database, the respondents would have had to click the "next" button on the survey and been advanced to Q32. We make the most conservative assumption, that respondents read Q32 and actively refused to answer it. Presumed active refusals also include respondents who because of their answers to Q30 were advanced to Q31, and Q31 was their last answered question. Again, in order for the data from Q31 to have been submitted, the respondents would have had to click the "next" button on the survey and been advanced to Q32. We make the conservative assumption that respondents read Q32 and actively refused to answer it.

Presumed passive refusals are those respondents who answered Q30, advanced to Q31 by the skip logic, and did not answer Q31. In this case, we make the assumption that because the respondents did not answer Q31, they did not see Q32.

Finally, respondents who answered questions after Q32, but did not answer Q32 are considered active refusals because it appears they intentionally skipped the question. We can calculate the number of active refusals in the following way:

1) DMDC knows that 3,748 partial respondents did not answer the USC question.

2) Drop-off analysis shows that 3,691 dropped out permanently at or before Q30/31 (answered 30/31 and stopped). Therefore 57 (3,748-3,691) respondents must have skipped Q32, answered more questions, and dropped out later.

3) Summing the 57 active refusals and the 43 presumed active refusals gives us a conservative number of 100 non-passive refusals (less than 0.5 % of the respondents).

The low number of drop-offs suggests that the sensitive nature of the question deterred few members from answering the USC question.

Figure 1.
USC Drop-Off Analysis Flow Chart

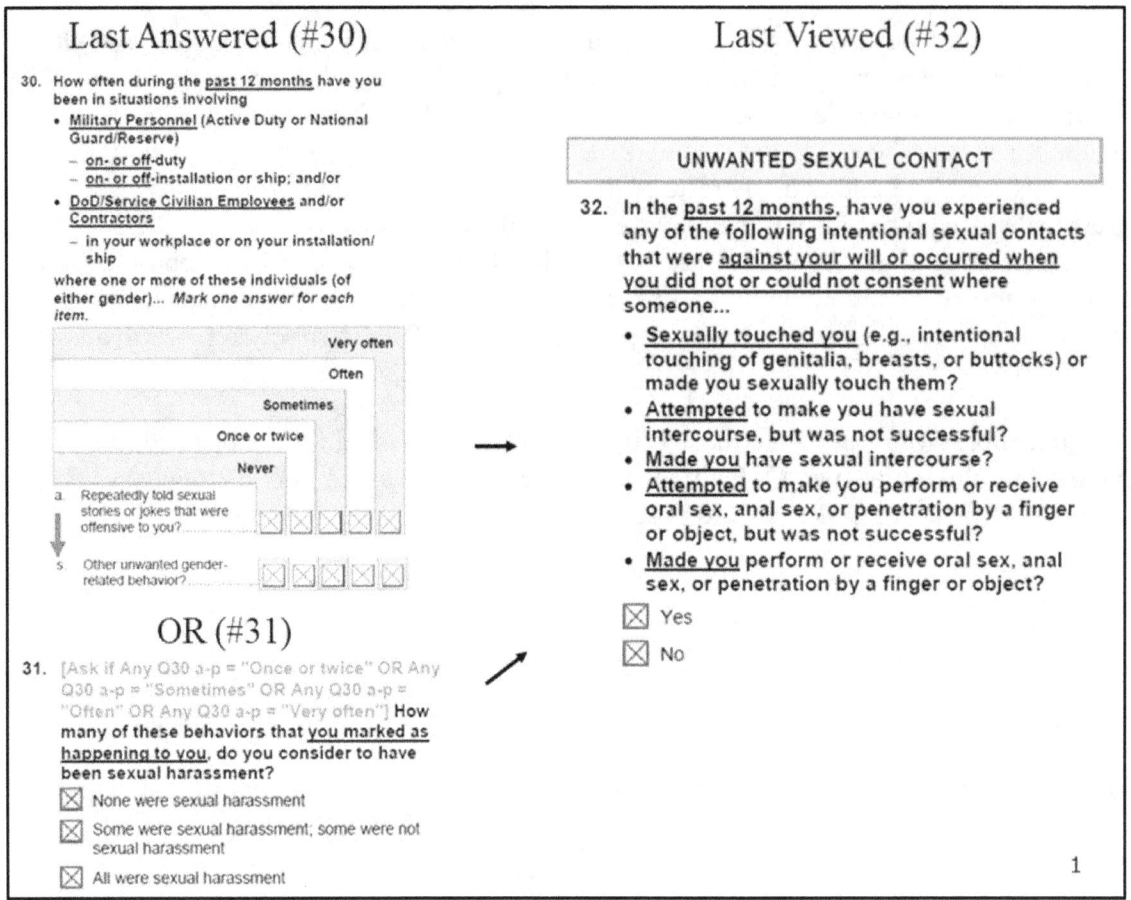

Further analysis of the drop-offs shows that an earlier question relating to PTSD caused the majority (698) of permanent drop-offs (last answered Q22j in Appendix B, Table B-1). A strong correlation between the two survey questions (PTSD and USC) may produce NRB if those who skip the PTSD question have different levels of PTSD, and consequently USC, than those who responded to the relevant questions. We checked the correlation, and WGRA respondents who report a USC incident also report much higher PTSD levels on Q23. Therefore, although the USC question appears to produce no direct NRB, there could be some NRB on the USC question indirectly related to prior drop-offs, if the drop-offs at PTSD are systematically different from members that continue the survey. Because of the focus of the survey is measuring sexual harassment and USC, a questionnaire design that moves these items earlier in the questionnaire will limit missing data for these questions. Because questionnaire design can have unexpected results for survey responses, we recommend conducting a randomized questionnaire-design experiment in a future WGRA where the USC question is asked earlier in the survey (before the PTSD question) to reduce the effect of item missing data as a source of NRB.

Summary of Analyzing Item Missing Data for USC Question

Similar to all DMDC surveys, unit missing data (members that fail to start the survey) is a much more severe problem than item missing data (skipping a question on the survey), but we investigated the item missing data for the USC question in search of potential NRB. The low number of drop-offs (100) when viewing the USC question provides evidence that the sensitive nature of the question did not deter members from answering the USC question and continuing the survey. The first of the set of questions on PTSD (Q23) produces the most drop-offs, and although PTSD is also a very sensitive question, the long series of scale questions (e.g., respondent burden) for both Q22 (stress) and Q23 (PTSD) seem the cause of missing data rather than the sensitivity of these questions. If the sensitivity were the major causal factor for missing data, we would expect missing data rates to vary greatly by the sensitivity of each sub-item a-q of Q23, but instead we find that most respondents stop the survey with sub-item a, likely because the task is too long. In summary, our analysis of missing data provides little evidence of NRB in USC estimates.

Section VII:
Analyze Whether Past USC Victims' Respond to Later WGRA Surveys at Different Rates

NRB occurs when survey respondents have different experiences than survey nonrespondents. DMDC has historical data to assess whether prior USC victims[18] respond to future WGRA surveys at different rates than non-victims. For example, if members who reported experiencing USC on the 2010 WGRA responded to the 2012 survey at significantly higher or lower rates than members who reported no USC experience, this may suggest NRB exists in WGRA 2012 USC estimates. For the NRB to occur, the effect of a 2-year old USC victimization on current survey response (e.g., 2010 victimization affecting 2012 response) would need to be similar to the effect of a recent victimization (within last 12 months) on response propensity to the current survey. Note that we cannot test this assumption with the data.

For each of three pairs of survey iterations available (2010 and 2012, 2006 and 2012, and 2006 and 2010), DMDC traced the distribution of members by Service, paygrade, and gender. The comparisons include the full sample from the earlier administration, the respondents from the earlier administration, and the members who answered the USC question in the earlier survey and were again sampled in the later survey. Table 18 shows these breakdowns for the 2010 and 2012 surveys, Table 19 shows the overlap from 2006 and 2012, and Table 20 shows the overlap from 2006 and 2010. For each comparison, the respondents from the earlier administration that were sampled again in the later administration are shown in total as well as broken down by their response to the USC question in the earlier administration (experienced USC or did not experience USC).

---

[18] Prior USC victims reported a USC experience on a previous administration of the survey.

Table 18.

Demographic Breakdown of the Overlap Between 2010 WGRA and 2012 WGRA

	2010 Sample		2010 Respondents		2010 Respondents Sampled in 2012		Experienced USC in 2010 and in 2012 Sample		Did Not Experience USC in 2010 and in 2012 Sample	
	Frequency	%	Frequency	%	Frequency	%	Frequency	%	Frequency	%
Total	85,614	100	24,029	100	2,575	100	95	100	2,480	100
Service[a]										
Army	25,788	30	6,703	28	400	16	18	19	382	15
Navy	18,682	22	5,330	22	346	13	17	18	329	13
Marine Corps	24,719	29	5,033	21	1,487	58	54	57	1,433	58
Air Force	16,425	19	6,963	29	342	13	6	6	336	14
Paygrade[b]										
E1-E4	46,981	55	7,706	32	965	37	59	62	906	37
E5-E9	21,885	26	8,243	34	723	28	12	13	711	29
W1-W5	3,690	4	1,642	7	104	4	1	1	103	4
O1-O3	7,816	9	3,462	14	546	21	21	22	525	21
O4-O6	5,242	6	2,976	12	237	9	2	2	235	9
Gender										
Male	54,673	64	14,000	58	608	24	5	5	603	24
Female	30,941	36	10,029	42	1,967	76	90	95	1,877	76

[a]Coast Guard was not included in the *2012 WGRA*, and therefore has been removed from this analysis.

[b]Members may have been promoted between the administrations of the 2010 and 2012 WGRA surveys. For consistency, the paygrade variable used is the 2010 administrative variable.

Table 19.

Demographic Breakdown of the Overlap Between 2006 WGRA and 2012 WGRA

	2006 Sample		2006 Respondents		2006 Respondents Sampled in 2012		Experienced USC in 2006 and in 2012 Sample		Did Not Experience USC in 2006 and in 2012 Sample	
	Frequency	%	Frequency	%	Frequency	%	Frequency	%	Frequency	%
Total	79,396	100	24,176	100	1,059	100	40	100	1,019	100
Service[a]										
Army	27,760	35	9,532	39	251	24	15	38	236	23
Navy	17,474	22	5,592	23	184	17	5	13	179	18
Marine Corps	17,356	22	3,070	13	494	47	16	40	478	47
Air Force	16,806	21	5,982	25	130	12	4	10	126	12
Paygrade[b]										
E1-E4	33,778	43	4,630	19	221	21	18	45	203	20
E5-E9	21,694	27	8,103	34	366	35	12	30	354	35
W1-W5	6,228	8	3,071	13	79	7	2	5	77	8
O1-O3	10,023	13	4,083	17	246	23	6	15	240	24
O4-O6	7,673	10	4,289	18	147	14	2	5	145	14
Gender										
Male	54,376	68	16,729	69	304	29	1	3	303	30
Female	25,020	32	7,447	31	755	71	39	98	716	70

[a]Coast Guard was not included in the 2012 WGRA, and therefore has been removed from this analysis

[b]Members may have been promoted between the administrations of the 2006 and 2012 WGRA surveys. For consistency, the paygrade variable used is the 2006 administrative variable.

Table 20.

Demographic Breakdown of the Overlap Between 2006 WGRA and 2010 WGRA

	2006 Sample		2006 Respondents		2006 Respondents Sampled in 2010		Experienced USC in 2006 and in 2010 Sample		Did Not Experience USC in 2006 and in 2010 Sample	
	Frequency	%	Frequency	%	Frequency	%	Frequency	%	Frequency	%
Total	86,213	100	26,505	100	1,871	100	37	100	1,834	100
Service										
Army	27,760	32	9,532	35	692	37	13	35	679	37
Navy	17,474	20	5,592	21	295	16	4	11	291	16
Marine Corps	17,356	20	3,070	11	383	20	12	32	371	20
Air Force	16,806	19	5,982	22	252	13	4	11	248	14
Coast Guard	6,817	8	2,691	10	249	13	4	11	245	13
Paygrade[a]										
E1-E4	36,295	42	5,200	19	138	7	10	27	128	7
E5-E9	24,971	29	9,499	35	485	26	11	30	474	26
W1-W5	6,316	7	3,129	12	504	27	2	5	502	27
O1-O3	10,482	12	4,402	16	308	16	10	27	298	16
O4-O6	8,149	9	4,637	17	436	23	4	11	432	24
Gender										
Male	60,122	70	15,865	60	1,029	55	2	5	1,027	56
Female	26,091	30	10,640	40	842	45	35	95	807	44

[a]Members may have been promoted between the administrations of the 2006 and 2010 WGRA surveys. For consistency, the paygrade variable used is the 2006 administrative variable.

Across the WGRA survey iterations the demographic subgroups female and junior enlisted are more likely to experience USC than other active duty members. For example, Table 20 shows that, 45% of the members who responded to the WGRA in 2006 and were later sampled in 2010 were females. However, 95% of the members in the 2010 sample who reported that they experienced USC in 2006 were female. The same table shows that junior enlisted (E1-E4) members comprised 7% of members who responded in 2006 and were sampled again for the later survey, but made up 27% of the members who reported USC and were sampled again. These relationships are consistent with the results in Table 18 and Table 19.

While demographic breakdowns differ based on prior reporting of experiencing USC, NRB will only result if the response rates for these subgroups differ between those who experienced USC and those who did not.

Because the number of members that 1) responded to a WGRA survey, 2) reported a USC, and 3) DMDC sampled in a subsequent WGRA is small (172), the margins of error around USC victims' response propensities (not shown) are large and all these analyses must be cautiously interpreted. Therefore we cannot show response propensities by demographic, but instead Table 21 shows the overall unweighted response propensities for later surveys by response to the earlier survey's USC question (columns).

Table 21.
Unweighted Response Propensity for Later Surveys Based on Prior USC

	Experienced USC in Earlier Survey, In Sample for Later Survey	Experienced USC in Earlier Survey, Responded to Later Survey	Percent Responding to Later Survey	Did Not Experience USC in Earlier Survey, In Sample for Later Survey	Did Not Experience USC in Earlier Survey, Responded to Later Survey	Percent Responding to Later Survey
2010 vs. 2012	95	35	37	2,480	1,112	45
2006 vs. 2012	40	16	40	1,019	535	53
2006 vs. 2010	37	19	51	1,834	1,102	60
Total	172	70	41	5,333	2,749	52

For all three pairs of surveys, members who did not report experiencing USC in the earlier survey, based on unweighted data, appear more likely to respond to the later survey (52% versus 41%). Two competing hypothesis for WGRA surveys are 1) USC victims are more likely to respond to "tell their story" or make the military aware of this serious problem, or 2) USC victims avoid this survey because it may cause them to re-experience a traumatic event. The data provides limited support for the latter hypothesis, and indicates USC rates may be underestimated because some USC victims participate at lower rates to future WGRA surveys. However, if these propensities are explained by demographic variables, the weighting may eliminate any nonresponse bias. For instance, some demographic subgroups that disproportionately experience USC, such as junior enlisted, are also traditionally poor respondents. Therefore, as described above, the lower response propensity for members who reported experiencing prior USC may be a result of their demographics rather than their USC experience. Because DMDC accounts for paygrade during weighting, the different response propensities by USC experience may be accounted for due to the correlation between paygrade and USC experience.

To further ensure that differences in WGRA response propensities are related to prior USC victimization and not simply demographics, DMDC ran logistic regression models where the dependent variable was response to the survey and independent variables were Service, paygrade, gender, education, family status (e.g., single with children), and a dummy variable for prior USC victimization. For six separate model runs (unweighted and weighted for each of the three comparison years [i.e., 2010 versus 2012]), the coefficient on the USC victimization variable was negative, indicating that after controlling for the other characteristics in the model, members with a prior USC experience were less likely to respond to a later WGRA survey. This provides additional evidence against the hypothesis that the WGRA survey overestimates USC rates because USC victims are more likely to take the survey.

Table 22 shows a weighted version of the prior table using the base weights from the later survey (inverse of selection probabilities). It is more appropriate to analyze weighted response rates because the weights account for differences in sample designs (as mentioned earlier, the 2012 survey has a much larger Marine Corps sample size). The weighted estimates are all in the same directions as the unweighted analysis, but the differences between USC victims and non-victims response propensities are larger in this table, showing that prior USC victims are much less likely to respond to a future WGRA survey (28% compared with 52%).

Table 22.
Weighted Response Propensity for Later Surveys Based on Prior USC

	Experienced USC in Earlier Survey, In Sample for Later Survey	Experienced USC in Earlier Survey, Responded to Later Survey	Percent Responding to Later Survey	Did Not Experience USC in Earlier Survey, In Sample for Later Survey	Did Not Experience USC in Earlier Survey, Responded to Later Survey	Percent Responding to Later Survey
2010 vs. 2012	453	99	22	17,818	8,322	47
2006 vs. 2012	223	68	30	11,707	6,046	52
2006 vs. 2010	199	74	37	18,697	10,890	58
Total	**875**	**241**	**28**	**48,222**	**25,258**	**52**

Summary of Analysis of Whether Past USC Victims' Respond to Later WGRA Surveys at Different Rates

To assess NRB, we checked whether USC victims may be more (or less) likely to respond than non-victims by tracing prior WGRA survey respondents that reported a USC to later studies and examining their response rates to the later study. There were 172 members (Table 16) that reported a USC and were sampled for a later WGRA. These members had lower response rates than non-victims to later surveys, potentially providing evidence that USC victims are less likely to respond to subsequent WGRA surveys. That is, based on our analysis, there is some evidence for NRB which would indicate the 2012 WGRA underestimated USC rate. However, we caution against drawing conclusions from this study alone due to the low number of prior USC victims, and because the prior victims are disproportionately female and junior enlisted, caused by the higher sampling rates and larger victimization rates for these subgroups.

Future Model-Based Research

DMDC will attempt to validate this result using other model-based approaches to NRB estimation, including (1) Heckman models to measure selection bias: (2) propensity score matching: (3) matching estimators; and (4) propensity score analysis with nonparametric regression. DMDC will conduct a comprehensive analysis of survey NRB by evaluating these model-based approaches to NRB estimation. This will include sensitivity analysis of the alternative approaches, and will enable DMDC to validate findings and potentially improve USC estimation.

References

Brick, J., and Bose, J. (2001). "Analysis of Potential Nonresponse Bias," Proceedings of the Survey Research Methods Section of the American Statistical Association. August 5-9, 2001.

DMDC. (2012a). *2012 Workplace and Gender Relations Survey of the Active Duty Members: Administration, datasets, and codebook* (Report No. 2012-068). Alexandria, VA.

DMDC. (2012b). *2012 Workplace and Gender Relations Survey of the Active Duty Members: Statistical methodology report* (Report No. 2012-067). Alexandria, VA.

DMDC. (2012c). *2012 Workplace and Gender Relations Survey of the Active Duty Members: Tabulation of responses.* (Report No. 2012-065). Alexandria, VA.

Groves, Robert M., and Cooper, M.P. (1998). Nonresponse in Household Interview Survey. New York: John Wiley & Sons, Inc.

Groves, Robert.M., and Peytcheva, E. (2008). "The Impact of Nonresponse Rates on Nonresponse Bias." A Meta-Analysis. Public Opinion Quarterly Vol. 72, pp. 167-189

Keeter, S., Miller, C., Kohut, A., Groves, R. M., and Presser, S. (2000). "Consequences of Reducing Nonresponse in a National Telephone Survey," Public Opinion Quarterly, 2, 125–148. [1, 2].

Levy, P., and Lemeshow, S. (1999). Sampling of Populations: Methods and applications. New York: J. Wiley and Sons.

Lin, I-Fen and Schaeffer, N.C. (1995). "Using Survey Participants to Estimate the Impact of Nonparticipation," Public Opinion Quarterly, Vol. 59, No. 2, pp. 236-258.

Appendix A.
Demographic Breakdown Between Complete and Partial Respondents

Demographic Breakdown Between Complete and Partial Respondents

Table A-1.

Unweighted Demographic Breakdown Between Complete, Partial Respondents and Active Refusals

Variable	Complete Respondents		Partial Respondents		Active Refusals	
	Frequency	Percent	Frequency	Percent	Frequency	Percent
Total	22,792	100	3,759	100	100	100
Satisfaction Level[a]						
Very dissatisfied	1,054	5	135	5	13	13
Dissatisfied	2,185	10	293	11	13	13
Neither satisfied nor dissatisfied	3,957	17	570	22	13	13
Satisfied	10,259	45	1,109	42	49	49
Very satisfied	5,304	23	511	20	11	11
Service						
Army	4,103	18	724	19	18	18
Navy	3,730	16	542	14	15	15
Marine Corps	10,416	46	1,846	49	47	47
Air Force	4,543	20	647	17	20	20
Paygrade						
E1-E3, Enlisted Unknowns	4,631	20	1,092	29	30	30
E4	3,592	16	762	20	24	24
E5-E6	6,526	29	1,053	28	21	21
E7-E9	2,590	11	310	8	5	5
W1-W5	631	3	47	1	4	4
O1-O3, Officer Unknowns	2,994	13	378	10	14	14
O4-O6	1,828	8	117	3	2	2
Education						
No college/Unknown	14,863	65	2,854	76	73	73
Some college	2,213	10	319	8	9	9
4-year degree or higher	5,716	25	586	16	18	18
Marital Status						
Not Married	9,709	43	1,915	51	49	49
Married/Unknown	13,083	57	1,844	49	51	51
Gender						
Male/Unknown	11,245	49	1,695	45	43	43
Female	11,547	51	2,064	55	57	57
Race/Ethnicity						
White/Unknown	14,329	63	1,959	52	51	51
Black	3,558	16	881	23	25	25
Hispanic	2,986	13	615	16	15	15
Other	1,919	8	304	8	9	9

[a]"Satisfaction Level" is the overall satisfaction with the military way of life (Q18). To allow better comparison of member satisfaction, we computed the percent in each category after removing members that had missing data on the satisfaction question (33 for complete respondents, 1,141 for partial respondents, and 1 from active refusals).

Appendix B.
Drop-Off Analysis

Drop-Off Analysis

How to read Drop-Off Analysis. For the *2012 WGRA* DMDC ran a macro to determine the last question that a potential respondent answered. Each row of the table shows the frequency of members dropping off after answering a particular question. For instance, the first row shows a frequency of 19 members dropping off after answering "Were you on active duty on September 17?" Those 19 members read and answered that question, but did not answer any subsequent questions. For the most part, the table can be read linearly, however it is important to note that skip patterns might exist for certain respondents. The furthest right column shows the aggregate percent of drop-offs as the survey progresses. Finally, Q91 or Q92 is considered the last question of the *2012 WGRA*, depending on which skip pattern members were selected in. Members that answered either Q91 or 92 are considered to have finished the survey.

Read row 1 of the drop-off analysis as 19 members answered Q1 and didn't answer another question on the survey. Therefore, when you see a large drop-off like the 107 on Q10, this table does not indicate that 107 members dropped off because they failed to answer the "gender" question; instead, it indicates that 107 people last answered the "gender" question, and were likely on the Web screen for Q11 "trust supervisor" when they stopped.

Table B-1.
Drop-Off Analysis

Last Question Answered	Question text	Sub item	Frequency	Cumulative Frequency	Cumulative Percent
1	Were you on active duty on September 17?	--	19	19	0.07
2	Are you...?	--	11	30	0.11
3	Are you Spanish/Hispanic/Latino?	--	28	58	0.22
4e	What is your race?	Native Hawaiian or other Pacific Islander (e.g., Samoan, Guamanian, or Chamorro)	36	94	0.35

Table B-1. (continued)

Last Question Answered	Question text	Sub item	Frequency	Cumulative Frequency	Cumulative Percent
5b	In the past 12 months, have you been deployed for any of the following operations?	Operation Iraqi Freedom/New Dawn	7	101	0.38
5c	In the past 12 months, have you been deployed for any of the following operations?	Other	57	158	0.60
6	In the past 12 months, have you been deployed to a combat zone or to an area where you drew imminent danger pay or hostile fire pay?	---	16	174	0.66
7	To what extent do/would you feel safe during deployments from being sexually assaulted on your base/installation/ship?	---	42	216	0.81
8	To what extent do/would you feel safe from being sexually assaulted on your home base/installation/ship?	---	29	245	0.92
9	Are you currently in a work environment where members of your gender are uncommon?	---	13	258	0.97
10	What is the gender of your immediate supervisor?	---	107	365	1.37
11a	How much do you agree or disagree with the following statements about your supervisor?	You trust your supervisor.	2	367	1.38
11b	How much do you agree or disagree with the following statements about your supervisor?	Your supervisor ensures that all assigned personnel are treated fairly.	3	370	1.39
11c	How much do you agree or disagree with the following statements about your supervisor?	There is very little conflict between your supervisor and the people who report to him/her.	2	372	1.40
11d	How much do you agree or disagree with the following statements about your supervisor?	Your supervisor evaluates your work performance fairly.	2	374	1.41
11e	How much do you agree or disagree with the following statements about your supervisor?	Your supervisor assigns work fairly in your work group.	6	380	1.43
11f	How much do you agree or disagree with the following statements about your supervisor?	You are satisfied with the direction/ supervision you receive.	292	672	2.53

Table B-1. (continued)

Last Question Answered	Question text	Sub item	Frequency	Cumulative Frequency	Cumulative Percent
12a	To what extent do you agree or disagree with the following statements about your work group?	If you make a request through channels in your work group, you know somebody will listen.	11	683	2.57
12b	To what extent do you agree or disagree with the following statements about your work group?	The leaders in your work group are more interested in looking good than being good.	8	691	2.60
12c	To what extent do you agree or disagree with the following statements about your work group?	You would go for help with a personal problem to people in your chain of command.	7	698	2.63
12d	To what extent do you agree or disagree with the following statements about your work group?	The leaders in your work group are not concerned with the way Service members treat each other as long as the job gets done.	7	705	2.66
12e	To what extent do you agree or disagree with the following statements about your work group?	You are impressed with the quality of leadership in your work group.	5	710	2.67
12f	To what extent do you agree or disagree with the following statements about your work group?	The leaders in your work group are more interested in furthering their careers than in the well-being of their Service members.	138	848	3.19
13a	How much do you agree or disagree with the following statements about the people in your work group?	There is very little conflict among your coworkers.	1	849	3.20
13b	How much do you agree or disagree with the following statements about the people in your work group?	Your coworkers put in the effort required for their jobs.	2	851	3.21
13c	How much do you agree or disagree with the following statements about the people in your work group?	The people in your work group tend to get along.	1	852	3.21
13e	How much do you agree or disagree with the following statements about the people in your work group?	You are satisfied with the relationships you have with your coworkers.	135	987	3.72

61

Table B-1. (continued)

Last Question Answered	Question text	Sub item	Frequency	Cumulative Frequency	Cumulative Percent
14a	How much do you agree or disagree with the following statements about the work you do at your workplace?	Your work provides you with a sense of pride.	3	990	3.73
14b	How much do you agree or disagree with the following statements about the work you do at your workplace?	Your work makes good use of your skills.	2	992	3.74
14c	How much do you agree or disagree with the following statements about the work you do at your workplace?	You like the kind of work you do.	3	995	3.75
14f	How much do you agree or disagree with the following statements about the work you do at your workplace?	Your day-to-day work is directly tied to your wartime job.	51	1046	3.94
15b	Overall, how well prepared...	Is your unit to perform its wartime mission?	25	1071	4.03
16a	Overall, how would you rate...	Your current level of morale?	2	1073	4.04
16b	Overall, how would you rate...	The current level of morale in your unit?	39	1112	4.19
17	Suppose that you have to decide whether to stay on active duty. Assuming you could stay, how likely is it that you would choose to do so?	---	16	1128	4.25
18	Overall, how satisfied are you with the military way of life?	---	177	1305	4.91
19a	How often during the past 12 months have you experienced any of the following behaviors where coworkers or supervisors...	Intentionally interfered with your work performance?	6	1311	4.94
19b	How often during the past 12 months have you experienced any of the following behaviors where coworkers or supervisors...	Did not provide information or assistance when you needed it?	2	1313	4.95
19c	How often during the past 12 months have you experienced any of the following behaviors where coworkers or supervisors...	Were excessively harsh in their criticism of your work performance?	1	1314	4.95
19e	How often during the past 12 months have you experienced any of the following behaviors where coworkers or supervisors...	Gossiped/talked about you?	1	1315	4.95
19f	How often during the past 12 months have you experienced any of the following behaviors where coworkers or supervisors...	Used insults, sarcasm, or gestures to humiliate you?	3	1318	4.96
19i	How often during the past 12 months have you experienced any of the following behaviors where coworkers or supervisors...	Damaged or stole your property or equipment?	48	1366	5.14

62

Table B-1. (continued)

Last Question Answered	Question text	Sub item	Frequency	Cumulative Frequency	Cumulative Percent
20a	How true or false is each of the following statements for you?	I am as healthy as anybody I know.	2	1368	5.15
20d	How true or false is each of the following statements for you?	My health is excellent.	31	1399	5.27
21a	Overall, how would you rate the current level of stress in your...	Work life?	3	1402	5.28
21b	Overall, how would you rate the current level of stress in your...	Personal life?	232	1634	6.15
22a	In the past month, how often have you...	Been upset because of something that happened unexpectedly?	6	1640	6.18
22b	In the past month, how often have you...	Felt that you were unable to control the important things in your life?	2	1642	6.18
22c	In the past month, how often have you...	Felt nervous and stressed?	6	1648	6.21
22d	In the past month, how often have you...	Felt confident about your ability to handle your personal problems?	4	1652	6.22
22e	In the past month, how often have you...	Felt that things were going your way?	2	1654	6.23
22f	In the past month, how often have you...	Found that you could not cope with all of the things you had to do?	3	1657	6.24
22g	In the past month, how often have you...	Been able to control irritations in your life?	1	1658	6.24
22i	In the past month, how often have you...	Been angered because of things that were outside of your control?	4	1662	6.26
22j	In the past month, how often have you...	Felt difficulties were piling up so high that you could not overcome them?	698	2360	8.89
23a	Below is a list of problems that people sometimes have in response to stressful experiences. Please indicate how much you have been bothered by the following in the past month.	Having repeated, disturbing memories, thoughts, or images of a stressful experience?	11	2371	8.93
23b	Below is a list of problems that people sometimes have in response to stressful experiences. Please indicate how much you have been bothered by the following in the past month.	Having repeated, disturbing dreams of a stressful experience?	8	2379	8.96

63

Table B-1. (continued)

Last Question Answered	Question text	Sub item	Frequency	Cumulative Frequency	Cumulative Percent
23c	Below is a list of problems that people sometimes have in response to stressful experiences. Please indicate how much you have been bothered by the following in the past month.	Suddenly acting or feeling as if a stressful experience were happening again (as if you were reliving it)?	6	2385	8.98
23d	Below is a list of problems that people sometimes have in response to stressful experiences. Please indicate how much you have been bothered by the following in the past month.	Feeling very upset when something reminded you of a stressful experience?	5	2390	9.00
23e	Below is a list of problems that people sometimes have in response to stressful experiences. Please indicate how much you have been bothered by the following in the past month.	Having physical reactions (e.g., heart pounding, trouble breathing, or sweating) when something reminded you of a stressful experience?	25	2415	9.10
23f	Below is a list of problems that people sometimes have in response to stressful experiences. Please indicate how much you have been bothered by the following in the past month.	Avoiding thoughts about or talking about a stressful experience or avoiding having feelings related to it?	5	2420	9.11
23g	Below is a list of problems that people sometimes have in response to stressful experiences. Please indicate how much you have been bothered by the following in the past month.	Avoiding activities or situations because they remind you of a stressful experience?	2	2422	9.12
23j	Below is a list of problems that people sometimes have in response to stressful experiences. Please indicate how much you have been bothered by the following in the past month.	Feeling distant or cut off from other people?	1	2423	9.13
23k	Below is a list of problems that people sometimes have in response to stressful experiences. Please indicate how much you have been bothered by the following in the past month.	Feeling emotionally numb or being unable to have loving feelings for those close to you?	7	2430	9.15
23n	Below is a list of problems that people sometimes have in response to stressful experiences. Please indicate how much you have been bothered by the following in the past month.	Feeling irritable or having angry outbursts?	1	2431	9.16
23o	Below is a list of problems that people sometimes have in response to stressful experiences. Please indicate how much you have been bothered by the following in the past month.	Having difficulty concentrating?	1	2432	9.16
23p	Below is a list of problems that people sometimes have in response to stressful experiences. Please indicate how much you have been bothered by the following in the past month.	Being "super alert" or "on guard"?	1	2433	9.16

Table B-1. (continued)

Last Question Answered	Question text	Sub item	Frequency	Cumulative Frequency	Cumulative Percent
23q	Below is a list of problems that people sometimes have in response to stressful experiences. Please indicate how much you have been bothered by the following in the past month.	Feeling jumpy or easily startled?	97	2530	9.53
24a	Over the past month, have you been bothered by the following problems?	Little interest or pleasure in doing things	2	2532	9.54
24b	Over the past month, have you been bothered by the following problems?	Feeling down, depressed, or hopeless	1	2533	9.54
24c	Over the past month, have you been bothered by the following problems?	Trouble falling or staying asleep, or sleeping too much	2	2535	9.55
24e	Over the past month, have you been bothered by the following problems?	Poor appetite or overeating	1	2536	9.55
24g	Over the past month, have you been bothered by the following problems?	Trouble concentrating on things, such as reading the newspaper or watching television	1	2537	9.55
24h	Over the past month, have you been bothered by the following problems?	Moving or speaking so slowly that other people could have noticed. Or the opposite — being so fidgety or restless that you have been moving around a lot more than usual	90	2627	9.89
25a	Were any of the problems you marked in the previous questions a result of experiencing...	Combat or being in a combat zone?	1	2628	9.90
25d	Were any of the problems you marked in the previous questions a result of experiencing...	Other traumatic military events?	1	2629	9.90
25f	Were any of the problems you marked in the previous questions a result of experiencing...	Traumatic events prior to entering military service?	8	2637	9.93
25g	Were any of the problems you marked in the previous questions a result of experiencing...	Other	143	2780	10.47

65

Table B-1. (continued)

Last Question Answered	Question text	Sub item	Frequency	Cumulative Frequency	Cumulative Percent
26a	How much do you agree or disagree with the following statements that might affect your decision to receive mental health counseling or service if you ever had a problem?	I don't know where to get help.	3	2783	10.48
26b	How much do you agree or disagree with the following statements that might affect your decision to receive mental health counseling or service if you ever had a problem?	I don't have adequate transportation.	2	2785	10.49
26e	How much do you agree or disagree with the following statements that might affect your decision to receive mental health counseling or service if you ever had a problem?	It would be too embarrassing.	1	2786	10.49
26f	How much do you agree or disagree with the following statements that might affect your decision to receive mental health counseling or service if you ever had a problem?	It would harm my career.	1	2787	10.50
26h	How much do you agree or disagree with the following statements that might affect your decision to receive mental health counseling or service if you ever had a problem?	My leaders might treat me differently.	8	2795	10.53
26j	How much do you agree or disagree with the following statements that might affect your decision to receive mental health counseling or service if you ever had a problem?	I would be seen as weak.	1	2796	10.53
26k	How much do you agree or disagree with the following statements that might affect your decision to receive mental health counseling or service if you ever had a problem?	Mental health care does not work.	1	2797	10.53
26l	How much do you agree or disagree with the following statements that might affect your decision to receive mental health counseling or service if you ever had a problem?	Mental health care counseling may impact my security clearance.	332	3129	11.78
27a	During the past 12 months, did any of the following happen to you? If it did, do you believe your gender was a factor?	You were rated lower than you deserved on your last military evaluation.	5	3134	11.80
27b	During the past 12 months, did any of the following happen to you? If it did, do you believe your gender was a factor?	Your last military evaluation contained unjustified negative comments.	10	3144	11.84
27c	During the past 12 months, did any of the following happen to you? If it did, do you believe your gender was a factor?	You were held to a higher performance standard than others in your military job.	4	3148	11.86

66

Table B-1. (continued)

Last Question Answered	Question text	Sub item	Frequency	Cumulative Frequency	Cumulative Percent
27d	During the past 12 months, did any of the following happen to you? If it did, do you believe your gender was a factor?	You did not get a military award or decoration given to others in similar circumstances.	6	3154	11.88
27e	During the past 12 months, did any of the following happen to you? If it did, do you believe your gender was a factor?	Your current military assignment has not made use of your job skills.	1	3155	11.88
27f	During the past 12 months, did any of the following happen to you? If it did, do you believe your gender was a factor?	Your current assignment is not good for your career if you continue in the military.	12	3167	11.93
27g	During the past 12 months, did any of the following happen to you? If it did, do you believe your gender was a factor?	You did not receive day-to-day, short-term tasks in your military job that would have helped you prepare for advancement.	5	3172	11.95
27h	During the past 12 months, did any of the following happen to you? If it did, do you believe your gender was a factor?	You did not have a professional relationship with someone who advised (mentored) you on military career development or advancement.	2	3174	11.95
27i	During the past 12 months, did any of the following happen to you? If it did, do you believe your gender was a factor?	You did not learn until it was too late of opportunities that would have helped your military career.	2	3176	11.96
27j	During the past 12 months, did any of the following happen to you? If it did, do you believe your gender was a factor?	You were unable to get straight answers about your military promotion possibilities.	5	3181	11.98
27l	During the past 12 months, did any of the following happen to you? If it did, do you believe your gender was a factor?	You did not get a military job assignment that you wanted and for which you were qualified.	3	3184	11.99
27m	During the past 12 months, did any of the following happen to you? If it did, do you believe your gender was a factor?	Have you had any other adverse personnel actions in the past 12 months?	213	3397	12.79
28	You answered "Yes, and your gender was a factor" to "You did not get a military job assignment that you wanted and for which you were qualified" above. Was this assignment legally open to women?	---	2	3399	12.80

Table B-1. (continued)

Last Question Answered	Question text	Sub item	Frequency	Cumulative Frequency	Cumulative Percent
29c	Do you consider ANY of the behaviors which you marked as happening to you in the previous question to have been...	Age discrimination?	1	3400	12.80
29d	Do you consider ANY of the behaviors which you marked as happening to you in the previous question to have been...	Religious discrimination?	13	3413	12.85
29e	Do you consider ANY of the behaviors which you marked as happening to you in the previous question to have been...	Other?	190	3603	13.57
30a	How often during the past 12 months have you been in situations involving ... where one or more of these individuals (of either gender)...	Repeatedly told sexual stories or jokes that were offensive to you?	8	3611	13.60
30b	How often during the past 12 months have you been in situations involving ... where one or more of these individuals (of either gender)...	Referred to people of your gender in insulting or offensive terms?	5	3616	13.62
30c	How often during the past 12 months have you been in situations involving ... where one or more of these individuals (of either gender)...	Made unwelcome attempts to draw you into a discussion of sexual matters (e.g., attempted to discuss or comment on your sex life)?	7	3623	13.64
30d	How often during the past 12 months have you been in situations involving ... where one or more of these individuals (of either gender)...	Treated you "differently" because of your gender (e.g., mistreated, slighted, or ignored you)?	1	3624	13.65
30e	How often during the past 12 months have you been in situations involving ... where one or more of these individuals (of either gender)...	Made offensive remarks about your appearance, body, or sexual activities?	5	3629	13.67
30f	How often during the past 12 months have you been in situations involving ... where one or more of these individuals (of either gender)...	Made gestures or used body language of a sexual nature that embarrassed or offended you?	6	3635	13.69
30g	How often during the past 12 months have you been in situations involving ... where one or more of these individuals (of either gender)...	Made offensive sexist remarks (e.g., suggesting that people of your gender are not suited for the kind of work you do)?	2	3637	13.70
30i	How often during the past 12 months have you been in situations involving ... where one or more of these individuals (of either gender)...	Put you down or was condescending to you because of your gender?	2	3639	13.71

Table B-1. (continued)

Last Question Answered	Question text	Sub item	Frequency	Cumulative Frequency	Cumulative Percent
30l	How often during the past 12 months have you been in situations involving … where one or more of these individuals (of either gender)…	Made you feel threatened with some sort of retaliation for not being sexually cooperative (e.g., by mentioning an upcoming review)?	2	3641	13.71
30n	How often during the past 12 months have you been in situations involving … where one or more of these individuals (of either gender)…	Intentionally cornered you or leaned over you in a sexual way?	1	3642	13.72
30o	How often during the past 12 months have you been in situations involving … where one or more of these individuals (of either gender)…	Treated you badly for refusing to have sex?	1	3643	13.72
30s	How often during the past 12 months have you been in situations involving … where one or more of these individuals (of either gender)…	Other unwanted gender-related behavior?	34	3677	13.85
31	How many of these behaviors that you marked as happening to you, do you consider to have been sexual harassment?	---	14	3691	13.90
32	In the past 12 months, have you experienced any of the following intentional sexual contacts that were against your will or occurred when you did not or could not consent where someone... Sexually touched you (e.g., intentional touching of genitalia, breasts, or buttocks) or made you sexually touch them? Attempted to make you have sexual intercourse, but was not successful? Made you have sexual intercourse? Attempted to make you perform or receive oral sex, anal sex, or penetration by a finger or object, but was not successful? Made you perform or receive oral sex, anal sex, or penetration by a finger or object?	---	62	3753	14.13
33	In the past 12 months, how many separate incidents of sexual touching, attempted or completed intercourse, oral or anal sex, or penetration by a finger or object did you experience? To indicate nine or more, select "9".	---	4	3757	14.15

69

Table B-1. (continued)

Last Question Answered	Question text	Sub item	Frequency	Cumulative Frequency	Cumulative Percent
34e	What did the person(s) do during the situation? Mark one answer for each behavior.	Made you perform or receive oral sex, anal sex, or penetration by a finger or object	9	3766	14.18
35h	Did the situation occur...	During Officer Candidate or Training School/Basic or Advanced Officer Course?	1	3767	14.19
37	What was/were the gender(s) of the offender(s)? Mark one.	---	8	3775	14.22
38a	Was the offender(s)...	Someone in your chain of command?	1	3776	14.22
40	Had either you or the offender(s) been drinking alcohol before the incident?	---	1	3777	14.22
41	Had either you or the offender(s) been using drugs before the incident?	---	3	3780	14.24
42c	Did the offender(s)...	Use some degree of physical force (e.g., holding you down)?	1	3781	14.24
44c	As a result of this situation, to what extent did...	Your work performance decrease?	1	3782	14.24
45	Did you report this situation to a civilian authority or organization?	---	1	3783	14.25
46	Did you report this situation to an installation/Service/DoD authority or organization?	---	13	3796	14.30
52	Was the criminal investigator(s) handling your report...	---	1	3797	14.30
59c	As a result of this situation, did you... Mark "Yes," "No," or "Don't know" for each item.	Experience any administrative actions (e.g., placed on a medical hold, placed on a legal hold, transferred to a different assignment)?	2	3799	14.31
59d	As a result of this situation, did you... Mark "Yes," "No," or "Don't know" for each item.	Experience any punishments for infractions/violations, such as underage drinking or fraternization?	1	3800	14.31
60g	How satisfied have you been with...	The reporting process overall?	2	3802	14.32
68e	When you reported the situation, were you offered...	Chaplain services?	3	3805	14.33

70

Table B-1. (continued)

Last Question Answered	Question text	Sub item	Frequency	Cumulative Frequency	Cumulative Percent
70	How long after the situation occurred did you report it? Mark one.	---	1	3806	14.33
72c	What were your reasons for not reporting the situation to any of the installation/Service/DoD authorities or organizations? Mark "Yes" or "No" for each statement.	You felt uncomfortable making a report.	1	3807	14.34
73	In retrospect, would you make the same decision about reporting if you could do it over?	---	5	3812	14.36
74a	In an effort to prevent sexual assault, please indicate how well your unit leadership....	Makes it clear that sexual assault has no place in the military.	1	3813	14.36
74e	In an effort to prevent sexual assault, please indicate how well your unit leadership....	Creates an environment where victims would feel comfortable reporting.	27	3840	14.46
75g	In your work group, to what extent... Mark one answer in each item.	Would people be able to get away with sexual assault if it were reported?	82	3922	14.77
76a	To what extent are you willing to...	Report a sexual assault?	3	3925	14.78
76c	To what extent are you willing to...	Step in and stop a situation that might lead to sexual assault?	2	3927	14.79
76d	To what extent are you willing to...	Encourage someone who has experienced sexual assault to seek counseling?	1	3928	14.79
76e	To what extent are you willing to...	Encourage someone who has experienced sexual assault to report it?	20	3948	14.87
77d	You indicated you would not encourage someone to report a sexual assault. What are your reasons? Mark "Yes" or "No" for each statement.	You think reporting would take too much time/effort.	1	3949	14.87
78b	At my installation/ship, there is a... Mark "Yes," "No," or "Don't know" for each item.	Sexual Assault Victims' Advocate to help those who experience sexual assault.	21	3970	14.95
79b	How satisfied have you been with the availability of information on...	How to file an unrestricted report?	11	3981	14.99
80	Have you had any military training during the past 12 months on topics related to sexual assault?	---	305	4286	16.14

Table B-1. (continued)

Last Question Answered	Question text	Sub item	Frequency	Cumulative Frequency	Cumulative Percent
81a	My Service's sexual assault training...	Provides a good understanding of what actions are considered sexual assault.	2	4288	16.15
81b	My Service's sexual assault training...	Teaches that the consumption of alcohol may increase the likelihood of sexual assault.	1	4289	16.15
81c	My Service's sexual assault training...	Teaches how to avoid situations that might increase the risk of being a victim of sexual assault.	1	4290	16.16
81e	My Service's sexual assault training...	Teaches how to obtain medical care following a sexual assault.	2	4292	16.16
81f	My Service's sexual assault training...	Explains the role of the chain of command in handling sexual assaults.	6	4298	16.19
81g	My Service's sexual assault training...	Explains the reporting options available if a sexual assault occurs.	1	4299	16.19
81i	My Service's sexual assault training...	Explains how sexual assault is a mission readiness problem.	1	4300	16.19
81j	My Service's sexual assault training...	Explains the resources available to victims (e.g., Safe Helpline).	32	4332	16.32
82b	In your opinion, how effective was the training you received in... Mark one answer in each item.	Explaining the difference between restricted and unrestricted reporting of sexual assault?	28	4360	16.42
83b	Are you aware of the following sources for understanding sexual assault prevention and response?	The Sexual Assault Prevention Web site (www.myduty.mil).	1	4361	16.42
83c	Are you aware of the following sources for understanding sexual assault prevention and response?	My installation's Sexual Assault Awareness Month programs.	18	4379	16.49

72

Table B-1. (continued)

Last Question Answered	Question text	Sub item	Frequency	Cumulative Frequency	Cumulative Percent
84	Are you aware that the Department of Defense has a live, one-on-one, confidential hotline called DoD Safe Helpline that provides sexual assault support worldwide and 24/7 to members of the DoD community via online, telephone, and texting services?	--	83	4462	16.80
85	How did you hear about the DoD Safe Helpline? Mark the one most useful source of information.	--	165	4627	17.43
86a	Are the following statements true or false?	When you are in a social setting, it is your duty to stop a fellow Service member from doing something potentially harmful to themselves or others.	13	4640	17.48
86b	Are the following statements true or false?	If you tell a Sexual Assault Response Coordinator (SARC) or Victims' Advocate (VA) that you were sexually assaulted, the SARC/VA is not always required to provide your name to your commander.	7	4647	17.50
86c	Are the following statements true or false?	Your communications with a SARC or VA are protected by the Victims' Advocate Privilege (MRE 514).	4	4651	17.52
86e	Are the following statements true or false?	If you are sexually assaulted, you can trust the military system to protect your privacy.	1	4652	17.52
86f	Are the following statements true or false?	If you are sexually assaulted, you can trust the military system to ensure your safety following the incident.	1	4653	17.52
86h	Are the following statements true or false?	If you are sexually assaulted, you can request a transfer and receive a response within 72 hours.	54	4707	17.73

73

Table B-1. (continued)

Last Question Answered	Question text	Sub item	Frequency	Cumulative Frequency	Cumulative Percent
87	Suppose you see a Service member, who you do not know very well, getting drunk at a party. Someone tells you that one of your coworkers is going to lead that Service member off to have sex. What are you most likely to do in this kind of situation? Mark one.	---	31	4738	17.84
89	Prior to your entry into the military, did you experience any of the following intentional sexual contacts that were against your will or occurred when you did not or could not consent where someone...	---	27	4765	17.95
	Sexually touched you (e.g., intentional touching of genitalia, breasts, or buttocks) or made you sexually touch them?				
	Attempted to make you have sexual intercourse, but was not successful?				
	Made you have sexual intercourse?				
	Attempted to make you perform or receive oral sex, anal sex, or penetration by a finger or object, but was not successful?				
	Made you perform or receive oral sex, anal sex, or penetration by a finger or object?				
90	Since the date you first joined the military, have you ever experienced any of the following intentional sexual contacts that were against your will or occurred when you did not or could not consent where someone...	---	54	4819	18.15
91	Sexually touched you (e.g., intentional touching of genitalia, breasts, or buttocks) or made you sexually touch them?	---	8,065	12884	48.52
92	Attempted to make you have sexual intercourse, but was not successful?	---	13,669	26553	100.00

74

REPORT DOCUMENTATION PAGE

Form Approved
OMB No. 0704-0188

1. REPORT DATE *(DD-MM-YYYY)*	2. REPORT TYPE	3. DATES COVERED *(From - To)*
31-01-2014	Final Report	August - November 2012

4. TITLE AND SUBTITLE

2012 Workplace and Gender Relations Survey of Active Duty Members: Nonresponse Bias Analysis Report

5a. CONTRACT NUMBER

5b. GRANT NUMBER

5c. PROGRAM ELEMENT NUMBER

6. AUTHOR(S)

Al-Nassir, Fawzi; Falk, Eric; Hung, Owen; Magazine, Shoshana; Markham, Timothy; Masui, Phil; McGrath, David; Schneider, Jeffrey

5d. PROJECT NUMBER

5e. TASK NUMBER

5f. WORK UNIT NUMBER

7. PERFORMING ORGANIZATION NAME(S) AND ADDRESS(ES)

Defense Manpower Data Center (DMDC)
4800 Mark Center Drive, Suite 04E25
Alexandria, VA 22350

8. PERFORMING ORGANIZATION REPORT NUMBER

Report No. 2013-059

9. SPONSORING/MONITORING AGENCY NAME(S) AND ADDRESS(ES)

Sexual Assault Response and Prevention Office
4800 Mark Center Drive
Alexandria, VA 22350

10. SPONSOR/MONITOR'S ACRONYM(S)

SAPRO

11. SPONSOR/MONITOR'S REPORT NUMBER(S)

12. DISTRIBUTION/AVAILABILITY STATEMENT

Available for public release; distribution unlimited.

13. SUPPLEMENTARY NOTES

14. ABSTRACT

The Defense Manpower Data Center (DMDC) conducted several studies to assess the presence of nonresponse bias in estimates from the 2012 Workplace and Gender Relations Survey of Active Duty Members (2012 WGRA). The objective of this research was to assess the extent of nonresponse bias for the estimated rate of unwanted sexual contact (USC rate) in the active duty military. The level of nonresponse bias (NRB) can vary for every question on the survey, but DMDC focused on the USC rate because this is the central question on the survey. Nonresponse bias occurs when survey respondents are systematically different from the nonrespondents. Nonresponse bias can occur with high or low survey response rates, but the decrease in survey response rates in the past decade has resulted in a greater focus on potential NRB. DMDC investigated the presence of nonresponse bias using many different methods, and this paper summarizes various methods and results.

15. SUBJECT TERMS

Survey, Nonresponse Bias, Unwanted Sexual Contact Rate, Sexual Assault, Sexual Harassment

16. SECURITY CLASSIFICATION OF:			17. LIMITATION OF ABSTRACT	18. NUMBER OF PAGES	19a. NAME OF RESPONSIBLE PERSON
a. REPORT	b. ABSTRACT	c. THIS PAGE	SAR	82	Falk, Eric
UU	UU	UU			19b. TELEPHONE NUMBER *(Include area code)* 571-372-1098

Reset

Standard Form 298 (Rev. 8/98)
Prescribed by ANSI Std. Z39.18

INSTRUCTIONS FOR COMPLETING SF 298

1. REPORT DATE. Full publication date, including day, month, if available. Must cite at least the year and be Year 2000 compliant, e.g. 30-06-1998; xx-06-1998; xx-xx-1998.

2. REPORT TYPE. State the type of report, such as final, technical, interim, memorandum, master's thesis, progress, quarterly, research, special, group study, etc.

3. DATES COVERED. Indicate the time during which the work was performed and the report was written, e.g., Jun 1997 - Jun 1998; 1-10 Jun 1996; May - Nov 1998; Nov 1998.

4. TITLE. Enter title and subtitle with volume number and part number, if applicable. On classified documents, enter the title classification in parentheses.

5a. CONTRACT NUMBER. Enter all contract numbers as they appear in the report, e.g. F33615-86-C-5169.

5b. GRANT NUMBER. Enter all grant numbers as they appear in the report, e.g. AFOSR-82-1234.

5c. PROGRAM ELEMENT NUMBER. Enter all program element numbers as they appear in the report, e.g. 61101A.

5d. PROJECT NUMBER. Enter all project numbers as they appear in the report, e.g. 1F665702D1257; ILIR.

5e. TASK NUMBER. Enter all task numbers as they appear in the report, e.g. 05; RF0330201; T4112.

5f. WORK UNIT NUMBER. Enter all work unit numbers as they appear in the report, e.g. 001; AFAPL30480105.

6. AUTHOR(S). Enter name(s) of person(s) responsible for writing the report, performing the research, or credited with the content of the report. The form of entry is the last name, first name, middle initial, and additional qualifiers separated by commas, e.g. Smith, Richard, J, Jr.

7. PERFORMING ORGANIZATION NAME(S) AND ADDRESS(ES). Self-explanatory.

8. PERFORMING ORGANIZATION REPORT NUMBER. Enter all unique alphanumeric report numbers assigned by the performing organization, e.g. BRL-1234; AFWL-TR-85-4017-Vol-21-PT-2.

9. SPONSORING/MONITORING AGENCY NAME(S) AND ADDRESS(ES). Enter the name and address of the organization(s) financially responsible for and monitoring the work.

10. SPONSOR/MONITOR'S ACRONYM(S). Enter, if available, e.g. BRL, ARDEC, NADC.

11. SPONSOR/MONITOR'S REPORT NUMBER(S). Enter report number as assigned by the sponsoring/ monitoring agency, if available, e.g. BRL-TR-829; -215.

12. DISTRIBUTION/AVAILABILITY STATEMENT. Use agency-mandated availability statements to indicate the public availability or distribution limitations of the report. If additional limitations/ restrictions or special markings are indicated, follow agency authorization procedures, e.g. RD/FRD, PROPIN, ITAR, etc. Include copyright information.

13. SUPPLEMENTARY NOTES. Enter information not included elsewhere such as: prepared in cooperation with; translation of; report supersedes; old edition number, etc.

14. ABSTRACT. A brief (approximately 200 words) factual summary of the most significant information.

15. SUBJECT TERMS. Key words or phrases identifying major concepts in the report.

16. SECURITY CLASSIFICATION. Enter security classification in accordance with security classification regulations, e.g. U, C, S, etc. If this form contains classified information, stamp classification level on the top and bottom of this page.

17. LIMITATION OF ABSTRACT. This block must be completed to assign a distribution limitation to the abstract. Enter UU (Unclassified Unlimited) or SAR (Same as Report). An entry in this block is necessary if the abstract is to be limited.